proclamation 2

Aids for Interpreting the
Lessons of the Church Year

Paul S. Minear
and
Harry Baker Adams

series a

editors: Elizabeth Achtemeier · Gerhard Krodel · Charles P. Price

FORTRESS PRESS   **PHILADELPHIA**

Library of Congress Cataloging in Publication Data (Revised)

Main entry under title:

Proclamation 2.

Consists of 24 volumes in 3 series designated A, B, and C which correspond to the cycles of the three year lectionary plus 4 volumes covering the lesser festivals. Each series contains 8 basic volumes with the following titles: Advent-Christmas, Epiphany, Lent, Holy Week, Easter, Pentecost 1, Pentecost 2, and Pentecost 3.

CONTENTS: [etc.]—Series C: [1] Fuller, R. H. Advent-Christmas. [2] Pervo, R. I., and Carl III, W. J. Epiphany.—Thulin, R. L. et al. The lesser festivals. 4 v.

1. Bible—Homiletical use. 2. Bible—Liturgical lessons, English.
[BS534.5.P76]   251   79–7377
ISBN 0–8006–4079–9 (ser. C, v. 1)

8565B81   Printed in the United States of America   1–4097

Contents

Editor's Foreword

This volume follows the pattern of its predecessors in this series. It provides exegetical commentary and homiletical interpretation for lessons appointed to be read in the new common lectionary during cycle A from the tenth to the nineteenth Sundays after Pentecost. In churches which use a sequence of liturgical colors, the conventional color during this middle third of the long summer season after Pentecost is green. The emphasis is on growth in Christian life.

Year A is the year of St. Matthew. During the ten Sundays covered by this volume our congregations hear most of the text of the First Gospel, from the parables of the kingdom of heaven at the end of chapter 13 to the parable of the two sons in chapter 21. Throughout, the focus is on the figure of Jesus as a teacher of righteousness and as a worker of miracles. His words and deeds lead to the numinous and controversial incident at Caesarea Philippi (Matt. 16:17–18) when Simon Bar-Jona confesses his faith in Jesus as the Christ, receives the blessing which Jesus invokes from heaven, and accepts his new name, Peter—the rock. The readings show us the way of the disciple en route to the kingdom.

Second Lessons (Epistles) consist of material from the end of Romans (chaps. 8—14) and from the beginning of Philippians (chaps. 1—2). Like the Gospel readings, these appear in the lectionary in the order in which they occur in the NT books themselves. The Epistles during this season, like the Gospels, are read "in course." Thus there is no necessary thematic connection between the Gospel pericope on a given Sunday and the reading from the Epistle which comes with it. It is a striking commentary on the fundamental unity of the gospel message that the authors of this volume have been able to point out so often and so persuasively common motifs underlying both readings.

OT lessons comprise a series of memorable and vivid passages from the historical books and from Isaiah, Jeremiah, and Ezekiel. These have been chosen because they illuminate one of the NT readings. This connection has also been fruitfully explored by our authors.

The texts during this season of the church year are rich fare for preachers who want to fulfill their function not as entertainers but as

proclaimers of the biblical message, and are willing to put themselves
under the discipline of the Word. This editor believes that the exegetical
and homiletical material in this commentary will be found a judicious
guide and ready help in this enterprise, and will enable those who attend
to it to preach "not themselves, but Jesus Christ as Lord, with themselves as your servants for Jesus' sake" (2 Cor. 4:5—adapted).

The exegetical parts of the volume have been prepared by Paul S.
Minear, distinguished New Testament scholar, leader of the ecumenical
movement, and Professor Emeritus of New Testament at Yale Divinity
School. He is the author of *Images of the Church in the New Testament,
Jesus and His People, To Die and to Live*, and many other volumes. The
homiletical material is the work of Harry Baker Adams, Associate Dean
and Professor of Pastoral Theology at Yale Divinity School, and author
of *Priorities and People*.

Alexandria, Va.   CHARLES P. PRICE

The Tenth Sunday after Pentecost

Lutheran	Roman Catholic	Episcopal	Pres/UCC/Chr	Meth/COCU
1 Kings 3:5–12	1 Kings 3:5, 7–12	1 Kings 3:5–12	1 Kings 3:5–12	1 Kings 3:5–12
Rom. 8:28–30	Rom. 8:28–30	Rom. 8:26–34	Rom. 8:26–30	Rom. 8:28–30
Matt. 13:44–52	Matt. 13:44–52 or Matt. 13:44–46	Matt. 13:31–33, 44–49a	Matt. 13:44–52	Matt. 13:44–52

EXEGESIS

First Lesson: 1 Kings 3:5–12. The use of lectionaries has many good points, but also some which are bad. One drawback is the fact that to be short enough for inclusion an extract must omit much that is necessary for understanding. The story of Solomon's dream is an example. A curious and diligent expositor must march off the map of the text in one of four directions.

In the first place, he may reread the whole story of Solomon as son of David and Bathsheba (2 Sam. 12:24), as the third king of Israel, and as a central figure in the fortunes of Israel in the tenth century B.C. To this end he should read at least the first eleven chapters of 1 Kings, and perhaps 1 Chron. 22—29 and 2 Chron. 1—9.

As a second line of march, an expositor may choose to study the period of the Deuteronomic reforms, when 1 Kings was written, some four centuries after the events narrated. The setting of the dream (3:1–4) clearly reflects one of those reforms, the effort to ban worship at Canaanite high places in order to centralize worship in the Jerusalem temple. Our story also reflects the acceptance of dreams as a normal mode by which God disclosed his will to prophets (Gen. 20:3; 28:12f.; 31:11; Num. 12:6).

As an alternative, an expositor may explore the later pictures of Solomon as the model wise man, to whom much of the Wisdom Literature of the OT was traced (Prov. 1:1–7; Eccles. 1:1, 16; Pss. 72, 127). His dream and prayer form a link in the development of that rich tradition, an instance of "the fear of the Lord" that is everywhere viewed as the beginning of wisdom.

7

Or, if the expositor is more interested in political theology, he may examine the implications of the dream for the political thinking of Israel. To be a king one must govern aright, and one cannot govern aright unless he is able to discern the difference between good and evil (v. 9). The story of the two harlots (3:16–18) shows the canny ability of Solomon to test the honesty of petitioners, and thereby to exercise justice.

Lacking the time or energy to march off the map, one may find in the map itself (these eight verses) several accents that characterize biblical faith: confidence in God's ability to rule through and over Israel's kings; the divine gift of wisdom that enables kings to rule justly; humility and teachability as prime qualifications of kingship; prayer as the meeting point of human wisdom and divine guidance. The story expresses the pervasive conviction that the story of Israel is the story of God's stead-fast love.

Second Lesson: Rom. 8:28–30. For centuries this segment from Paul's thought has touched off explosive dogmatic quarrels, controversies for which the term *predestination* has been the fuse. Quarrels have often centered on the claim that some persons are permanently superior to others through being among God's elect. Every reader must try to avoid the fatal suction of those old quarrels by returning the verses to their original context.

What was the situation in Rome that Paul was opposing? In the Roman churches, some Jewish believers (7:1ff.) judged that gentile believers were permanently inferior unless and until they obeyed the scriptural demands for purity (14:1—15:13). Paul denied that inferiority. The only thing that mattered to him was whether Gentiles had been truly called by God. If God has in fact called them, he will himself make them conform—not to some human standard of behavior—but to "the image of his Son." All whom he has called are assured a place in his own glory. To accuse them of inferiority is to make oneself God's enemy. An adequate indication of God's call is provided by the fact of a person's praying, however clumsy or ignorant his prayer may be (vv. 26–27).

What permanent theological issue is at stake in these verses? The subject, who is active in man's faith. Notice that the subject in almost every verse is God. It is God who originates faith. Believers enter the story as objects of God's concern. Before a believer believes, God has acted. This is the force of the prefixes: *fore*knowledge, *pre*destination, and so forth. These prefixes force us to think of a time before the present. Our minds must move back, back, back to a mysterious primal time hidden in the depths of God's desiring. We must think of the connections between all human calendars and God's time, between our inclusion in God's family and the original source of that family. When Paul speaks of glorification, he has in mind the primeval glory that surrounds the Creator of All Things. When he speaks of the children of God, he has in mind the image of humanity before sin polluted the stream of history. Is that image to be seen in Jesus? If so, the basic question is not the relative status of various human groups (us versus them), but God's power to create a new humanity that fulfills his original purposes. These verses should serve as a fuse, not for igniting explosive debates, but for lighting candles of quiet confidence.

Gospel: Matt. 13:44–52. Matthew separated these parables into two groups: Some are addressed to the crowds (vv. 1, 34) but others to the disciples (vv. 10, 36). Whom did these groups represent in Jesus' day? The crowds are followers of Jesus who accepted his authority and benefited from his work of healing, feeding, and teaching; the disciples are those being trained for later work of healing, feeding, and teaching. But whom did the two groups represent in the churches for which Matthew was writing? The crowds would probably be identified with the lay members, and the disciples with the leaders (though, of course, we should not read back the modern pattern of a single pastor for each congregation). It is to these leaders that the last three parables are addressed, as a step in their training.

When Jesus asked them if they were able to grasp the secrets of the kingdom, they replied *yes*. Was that answer right or wrong? A leader who thinks that understanding is easy, and that he in fact does understand, may have totally failed to catch the deeper meanings. What kind of ears are needed? (v. 43). One thing is clear from the parables. Entrance into the kingdom is viewed as an unimaginable glory, as a reason for the greatest joy. This gift has greater value than anything else within human reach, and exclusion brings terrible agony and dereliction (v. 50). The parables make that self-evident. What is not self-evident is how to find this kingdom. Where is it? How does a person enter it? If I do not receive the joy, have I any right to an understanding? There are vast mysteries here, before which modesty must bow.

The kingdom is like . . . but like what? Like the treasure? like God's act in hiding it? like the field which must first be bought? like the surprise of discovery? like the forced sale of all other possessions? like the purchase of the field? Or is it like the accompanying joy? To make sense of this parable, where must I stand to be able to say "Yes, I understand it"? To convey the meaning of the parables to church members, where must the church leader stand?

The last parable, the story of the fish net, carries the matter a step further. Here the approach of the kingdom surprises the disciples not with joy but with terror. In training his apprentices, Jesus tried to make clear the options: inexpressible joy or shattering dread. Two or three generations later Matthew believed that an understanding of those options was necessary to qualify leaders of the churches.

HOMILETICAL INTERPRETATION

The three passages in the lectionary for this Sunday share a number of themes which can be identified and related to the situation in which persons today find themselves: an expression of the goal toward which life under God is directed; a statement of the gifts of God; a consideration of the context in which human existence is carried on; an affirmation of the decisive ways of God in the life of this world. One way of looking at the relationship of these three texts is to see in all of them a fundamental and creative theological tension between the affirmation of the absolute and decisive priority of God in human affairs, and the pressing necessity for persons to play a crucial role in their relationship with God. In each of the texts God is described as taking the initiative in what happens. He establishes Solomon as the king. He predestines those whom he is to call and justify and glorify. He puts the treasure in the field and creates the pearl of great price. Yet those who know and receive the gifts of God are not merely passive objects of God's work or inert vessels into which his gifts are poured. In every instance those whom God deals with are called to critical and creative response to what God is doing in them and through them.

First Lesson: 1 Kings 3:5–12. "At Gibeon the Lord apeared to Solomon in a dream by night; and God said, 'Ask what I shall give you.'" To be confronted with that offer by God is like having an X-ray taken of the soul. What is it we want God to do for us? The answer we make discloses what we value, what we discern to be the fulfillment of life on this earth, what we take to be genuinely significant in our lives.

Solomon's response to the Lord's offer was to ask for wisdom, a request that pleased God greatly. God indicated that he would give Solomon what he asked because he had asked for wisdom rather than some of the things he might have pleaded for: "long life or riches or the life of your enemies." It was important for Solomon to know what to ask for, as it is central in our relationship with God to know what to ask of him.

What enabled Solomon to ask rightly of God? How do we come to be able to ask rightly of God? Several things in Solomon's situation might be noted which have pertinence for how we can ask rightly of God. First, he was aware of what God had done in the past: "Thou hast shown great and steadfast love to thy servant David my father." Second, he knew that he was where he was by the grace and the power of God: "Thou has made thy servant king in place of David my father." As the first chapters of 1 Kings make clear, Solomon had not been entirely passive in the struggle for the throne after the death of David, and yet he had a clear sense that the responsibilities of the position had been entrusted to him by God.

Third, he was aware of his own need: "I am but a little child; I do not know how to go out or come in." He was deeply aware of the magnitude of the position which he had to fill and of the responsibilities which he had to bear. Finally, he was conscious that others were dependent upon him: "And thy servant is in the midst of thy people whom thou has chosen." What he asked of God was not for his personal gain but that he might be equipped to care for those entrusted to him.

God had set Solomon upon the throne of David, but because Solomon knew what to ask of God he brought blessing to himself and to his people.

Second Lesson: Rom. 8:28–30. The exegetical commentary points out the risk in this passage from Paul. When any people, then or now, think of themselves as predestined by God, called of God, justified before God, glorified by God, they are tempted to believe that they are better than others. Paul's words do not have to be so interpreted, and this brief segment from his thought does speak to our situation as we reflect on our relationship with God. The passage makes the point emphatically that life is not under our control. We have not ordained that we shall be, and we do not finally control our own destiny. To be sure the decisions we make are real decisions and have significant impact on us and others, but there is another Power at work shaping our destiny and the destiny of our world.

The passage makes us aware of God's call to us, of the reality that our relationship with God is not self-generated. We do not simply create faith and love by an act of God. As we think of how it has happened for us, we remember persons who have spoken a word, or a community which has borne witness, and these have brought forth faith within us. The passage articulates with helpful clarity that for which we have been predestined and called. Paul didn't talk about persons being predestined to a certain career, or to a level of success, or to a particular moment of death. They are "predestined to be conformed to the image of his Son." Those who are able to express something of the spirit and love of Jesus Christ in their lives are realizing what God has ordained for them.

Those who are so predestined are not simply passive objects being used by God. "God works for good with those who love him." To love God is our response, a response which we must make out of who we are. We love God because we have been loved by God, because in his love he has predestined us to share in the quality of life expressed in Jesus Christ. But love is not an automatic response. We love because we choose to seek to express our concern and care.

Gospel: Matt. 13:44–52. What kind of "yes" is it the disciples speak in v. 51? There can be a yes spoken with great confidence and absolute certainty; there can be a yes spoken with diffidence and hesitation. We do not know for certain what force the yes of the disciples carries, but most of us would not answer Jesus' question, "Have you understood all this?" with a resounding and unambiguous yes. We are just not sure what ought to be stressed in these parables. We find ourselves impressed with the rich and varied possibilities, but unwilling to make dogmatic assertions about what Jesus must have meant by telling these stories. But even without absolute certainty, we must venture to relate these anecdotes of Jesus to our own situation, and to risk our yes when Jesus asks if we have understood all this.

If the primary stress in the Second Lesson from Paul was on the prior purpose and action of God, the primary attention in the parables of the treasure and the pearl seems to be on the response of those who found these valuables. From one point of view their actions look like those of a fanatic. They give up everything else in order to gain the thing which they believe to be of surpassing value. Surely the parables are saying that the Kingdom of God is a treasure to be taken seriously. They certainly speak against a casual nonchalance about the whole business. The kingdom, the way of God, is a treasure to be cherished, to be prized, above all else. The line between disciplined attention and fanatical obsession is impossible to draw, but the way of God does demand the investment of attention and energy. Does seeking the treasure of the kingdom mean compulsive participation in the church? No, but it does mean serious involvement with the people of God. Does seeking the pearl of great value mean excluding everything not connected with religion? No, but it does mean earnest concern for the will of God in our world.

The stress in the parables is not on what has to be given up in order to gain the kingdom, but on the great value to be grasped in our relationship with God, a relationship which brings great joy to those who enter into it.

The Eleventh Sunday after Pentecost

Lutheran	Roman Catholic	Episcopal	Pres/UCC/Chr	Meth/COCU
Isa. 55:1–5	Isa. 55:1–3	Neh. 9:16–20	Isa. 55:1–3	Neh. 9:16–20
Rom. 8:35–39	Rom. 8:35, 37–39	Rom. 8:35–39	Rom. 8:31–39	Rom. 8:31–39
Matt. 14:13–21	Matt. 14:13–21	Matt. 14:13–21	Matt. 14:13–21	Matt. 14:13–21

EXEGESIS

First Lesson: Neh. 9:16–20. Every preacher knows how his thought suffers when a reporter lifts out of a carefully constructed sermon a few sentences for quotation in a newspaper. Therefore he should be alert to the violence done to Ezra's sermon by relying on only these excerpted sentences. A long, long story preceded the occasion Ezra faced. As priest and scribe he was addressing all the people after their return from Exile, and after restoration of worship in the temple. Having separated themselves from foreigners, this community gathered in solemn assembly to listen to God's law, to confess their sins, and to rejoice in their redemption. It was a formal celebration that required the most inclusive recital of God's wonderful deeds, of which not the least had been the Exodus from Egypt, and God's guidance of the pilgrimage through the wilderness (9:9–15). Though we could (and should) review the entire sermon, here we must focus upon the five verses in which are imbedded four motifs that are as basic to the NT as to the OT.

1. All disobedience to God is rooted in arrogance and presumption. Whenever a people claims credit for its own achievement, as, for example, its political independence, it has forgotten all the things God has done for its well-being in previous generations. It develops a "stiff neck"; its pride breeds refusal to obey.

2. When it worships, God's people should recall not so much its recent bondage in Babylon and its return to the land of promise, as that much earlier bondage in Egypt and the ancient wanderings in the wilderness. Whether they live as aliens in Babylon or as citizens in Judea, they continue to face the very choices that Israel faced during the forty years in the wilderness. That archetypal time of testing remains the perennial time of worship, when ultimate decisions are made.

3. The central decision, now as much as then, is whether to worship the God who gave them freedom or to make for themselves a golden calf. Blasphemy still takes the same form: To make a golden calf and to say to it: "*This* is your God who brought you up out of Egypt" (v. 18). The wilderness remains home for God's people, where it either attributes its freedom to its own abilities (the golden calf) or recognizes its total dependence on God for his mercy and grace (v. 17).

4. Ezra understands that worship transforms the ancient mercies of God into a fully contemporary resource. By worshiping God, Israel becomes aware again of living in the wilderness, sustained from day to day by manna and water, guided again by the twin pillars, instructed again by the same Spirit. God is as loathe to forsake his people now as he was then. True freedom, whether from Egypt or from Babylon, is granted in worship as a gift from this God; it is this freedom that actually separates Israel from foreigners (9:2). In worshiping the same God as Moses, the church in the NT would later inhabit the same wilderness.

Second Lesson: Rom. 8:31–39. This text needs to be saved from its admirers who so frequently quote it and as frequently abuse it. We misuse it whenever we drench it with sentimentality—when we treat Paul chiefly as a great orator speaking with his most dramatic rhetoric. We repeat each of his questions with our own best flair and flourish, transforming his harsh logic into a security blanket for timid Christians.

To destroy such sentimental handling we should first look at v. 36, which is not so much a pious thought but a photograph of brutal facts. (The whole of Psalm 44, from which this verse is taken, provides background.) Paul and his companions were suffering constant and hazardous persecution (read 2 Cor. 11:23–28). They were being scorned by their peers as no better than sheep, fit only for slaughter. We should realize that public contempt can be more painful than physical injury, especially when it is respected religious leaders who do the scoffing. There is nothing oratorical or sentimental about suffering, not even when it is the fruit of devotion to Christ. So each of the questions in vv.

31–35 springs from a desperate urgency. Were these martyrs servants of the devil, as their powerful enemies were saying, or were they servants of God? Perhaps they were simply misguided dupes. What gave Paul his confidence that they were not?

First, Paul knew that he and his companions had accepted suffering "for your sake" and out of love for Christ. This meant that "peril and sword" actually united them to Christ in his love for them. Death for him established unbreakable solidarity with Him in His death "for us."

Second, by raising Jesus from the dead God has declared his own love for Jesus and his own approval of Christ's love for us. Our love for Christ, expressed by enduring "tribulation or distress" for his sake, binds us to God's love and Christ's love for us.

And finally, the God who loved us is the Creator of All Things, standing at the beginning and the end of all things. Nothing that intervenes between that beginning and that ending, not even things to come, not even "death or life," can stand between us and him. So for Paul the grim facts of violence and hatred which appeared to be proofs of separation are instead proof of God's power. That very logic impelled him to sing a song of defiance to his enemies, not, "We shall overcome," but, "We are more than conquerors through . . ."

Gospel: Matt. 14:13–21. All three texts for this Sunday locate God's people in the wilderness. In the First Lesson, Israel's worship is seen as a perennial reminder of God's care during the long pilgrimage. Paul's situation in Romans (the Second Lesson) is one of famine and distress. Now in the Gospel followers of Jesus find themselves hungry and helpless in a lonely place, where they receive manna from the Messiah whose compassion is the means by which God turns scarcity into abundance. In the preceding paragraph the death of John provides an ominous prelude. That death prompts Jesus to withdraw to the desert, but it does not dissuade the crowds from following him there.

As Matthew retold the story for his readers, he blended together two situations, one in Jesus' day and the other in Matthew's. In the first, Jesus was the mediator between God's compassion and the sick (v. 14) and hungry crowds. Like Moses, Jesus was able to provide manna, a miracle that linked this situation to the deliverance from Egypt. When Jesus blessed and broke and gave the loaves, God was answering the familiar prayer: "Give us this day . . ." The line of service which enabled all to eat and to be satisfied ran from God through Jesus to the followers.

In Matthew's day, wilderness hunger and isolation is still the setting, though now the people are dependent upon those who had been trained by Jesus to feed them. Now their role in the story becomes more central. The command of Jesus for them to feed the crowds shifts the center of gravity from the reliance of the crowds (the laity) on Jesus to the responsibility of their leaders, who can now appreciate the transformation of their meagre resources to food ample for a huge multitude. Each of them gathers a basket of crumbs much larger than the whole he had to start with, symbolic of what happened whenever the church gathered for its eucharistic meal. Wilderness, or the rural setting for Psalm 23, is a fitting locale for such a miracle.

Such an understanding of Matthew's story is not wholly adequate. Many questions remain. But it illustrates a sound principle of interpretation. The reader of a story should try to be as imaginative as the teller, and as alert to sensing the overtones in the symbolic language. In this case, the dominant overtones echo from implicit references to the deliverance from Egypt and to the celebration of the Eucharist on the part of a persecuted community.

HOMILETICAL INTERPRETATION

Certainly the wilderness is a fitting symbol for the situation in which many people find themselves. In the biblical witness, the events of the escape of the people of Israel from their slavery in Egypt and the subsequent forty years of wandering in the wilderness were central in the understanding of this people and God's relationship with them. All of us can discern life related to an image which suggests that one is lost or threatened or suffering.

To see life in terms of persons in the wilderness uses a symbol which has a richness and complexity of meaning, and therefore which does some justice to the richness and complexity of human existence. The case can certainly be argued that the very conditions of life on this earth mean that there are going to be times of struggle and anguish for every person. Great achievements are not won without struggle. When God freed the people of Israel from their bondage in Egypt, Moses did not lead them via an interstate highway to their new home in the promised land. He led them into the wilderness. And that is simply the way life is.

Ezra talks of the way in which those who were led out of Egypt and those whom he calls "our fathers" acted arrogantly and disobeyed God, and "were not mindful of the wonders which thou didst perform among them." God had heard the cry of the people in their slavery, he had performed signs and wonders to force the Pharaoh to release them, he had divided the Red Sea so they could cross it, he had led them by a pillar of cloud by day and a pillar of fire by night. He had given them "right ordinances and true laws, good statutes and commandments" at Mount Sinai, he had given them bread from heaven and water from the rock. And yet the people were not mindful of what God had done and was doing for them. We may experience life as frustrating and frightening because we are unmindful of what God is doing to provide for us through his creation, to care for us through the loving concern of others, to sustain us through the presence of his Spirit.

Again, there are times when people are driven into the wilderness because they have made significant commitments which involve them in awesome struggles and sacrifices. The exegetical section points out the situation in which Paul found himself when he wrote his letter to the Romans. Paul's life would have doubtless been less tumultuous if he had not been so thoroughly caught up in the ministry of Jesus Christ. It was because of his commitment to Christ and his love for Christ's people that the words of the psalmist had such direct pertinence for his own life. In truth, faithfulness to the purpose of God will lead us to share the burdens of others and to get into the struggles of the oppressed and to protest the injustices done to people. All of these involvements may well lead us through experiences which can accurately be characterized as wandering in the wilderness.

Finally, there are times when people find themselves in the wilderness because life pounds them with terrible catastrophe. "Now when Jesus heard this, he withdrew from there in a boat to a lonely place apart." The "this" in that sentence is the brutal killing of John the Baptist at the behest of an angry woman whom John had offended. The death of the one who had predicted his coming and baptized him must have profoundly moved Jesus, for he withdrew from his ministry and sought a lonely place. Surely persons confront the possibilities of such tragedies that they will be shaken loose from all the structures of life and driven into lonely isolation.

If God does not spare us the wilderness, he also does not forsake us in the wilderness. Each of the texts affirms the promise of God to his people. The people of Israel were blessed and led by God as they made their long journey from the bondage of Egypt to the freedom of the land which God had promised. God gave them Moses to lead them. God gave them the pillars of cloud and fire to guide them. God gave them the ordinances and statutes and commandments to order their lives. God gave them the bread from heaven and the water from the rock to nourish them.

Because they were not mindful of the gifts of God, they became presumptuous and disobeyed God. They made a golden calf to worship, and tried to find somebody who would take them back to the security of their slavery in Egypt. Even with that provocation, even when they had created their own wilderness of rebellion against God, he did not forsake them. Ezra makes this striking affirmation of the character of God who will not give up on his people, whatever wilderness they have been driven to or whatever wilderness they have created for themselves. He calls Israel and us to the worship of the God who still guides and sustains his people. He calls Israel and us to be mindful of the wonders which God is yet doing.

Paul certainly knew desperate moments in his life. Out of his own intense experience of the wilderness Paul could affirm with an absolute confidence that nothing "will be able to separate us from the love of God in Christ Jesus our Lord." Paul grounds his confidence in the love which God expressed as he gave up his own Son for us, and in the triumph of love as Christ was raised from the dead. We live in the promise of God that nothing can separate us from his love because Jesus Christ has brought that love to us as he shared our life and our death, and because the risen Lord still manifests God's love as he intercedes for us.

Finally, Jesus and the disciples found themselves in the wilderness, but not alone there. There was a crowd with them, but that only compounded the difficulty for the crowd waited expectantly to be fed. Jesus suggested to the disciples that they feed the crowd. He said to them: "You give them something to eat." When the disciples responded that they had no resources to feed such a crowd, Jesus took what they had and blessed it and provided an abundance for all. The disciples were setting limits. They had no obligation to feed these people who had invited themselves to follow Jesus when he had sought to be alone. But Jesus pushed through the limit which says there are some people we don't have to care for and some needs we don't have to meet. Then Jesus pushed through the limit which says that we don't see how we can do what needs to be done. He took what seemed so inadequate and provided what was needed. Through the blessing which Christ gives to us he makes possible the blessing through us to others.

The Twelfth Sunday after Pentecost

Lutheran	Roman Catholic	Episcopal	Pres/UCC/Chr	Meth/COCU
1 Kings 19:9–18	1 Kings 19:9, 11–13a	Jon. 2:1–9	1 Kings 19:9–16	1 Kings 19:9–18
Rom. 9:1–5	Rom. 9:1–5	Rom. 9:1–5	Rom. 9:1–5	Rom. 9:1–5
Matt. 14:22–33	Matt. 14:22–33	Matt. 14:22–33	Matt. 14:22–33	Matt. 14:22–33

EXEGESIS

First Lesson: 1 Kings 19:9–18. This story marks a turning point in Elijah's struggle to defend God's altar against a triple threat. There had been collusion between King Ahab, Queen Jezebel, and the prophets of Baal whom Jezebel had persuaded Ahab to worship. Although Elijah had single-handedly won his contest with 450 of those prophets, Jezebel had sworn to have the victor killed. So he fled to Horeb, the mountain where God had sealed his covenant with his original servant, Moses. There God surprised Elijah, and the story surprises its readers, with unexpected questions and commands.

Twice God asks: "What are you doing here?" The implication is clear: "This is no place for you. Fear of death should not drive my spokesmen to use a cave on this mountain as a hiding place. Your place is back on the battlefield."

So Elijah finds God a stronger adversary than Jezebel or Baal. Twice he defends his flight to Horeb by pointing to quite obvious facts: His enemies are out to kill him; he has been defending God's altars; God's people have forsaken the covenant sealed on this very mountain. But God refused to accept any of these excuses. The sins of others provide no alibi sufficient to excuse Elijah's flight. (The Bible knew all about our ways of rationalizing guilt long before Freud.)

However, God did more than disclose Elijah's guilt. He issued the command "Go!" The refugee must return to the battlefield where he had supposed that God had lost control. In fact, God would now display his authority to replace one king by another, and one spokesman by another. To Elijah's self-pitying "I, even I only, am left," God responded with the declaration that he had left no fewer than seven-thousand faithful servants. (Both symbols, seven and a thousand, signified completeness, adequacy, and even perfection.)

God went even further and rubbed the lesson in by ordering Elijah to take the initiative in anointing a successor. But as Elijah returned to carry out this order, he was supported by memories, not of noisy tornado or shattering earthquake but of a quiet persuasive voice.

Second Lesson: Rom. 9:1–5. The three readings for this Sunday reflect common motifs. Paul's situation in Rom. 9—11 is not unlike that of Elijah's; he has suffered so much hostility from his kinsmen that he has been tempted to give them up. But he refused. He tells of his "unceasing anguish" for them. Few American Protestants share that anguish, for we are almost wholly Gentiles, untroubled by the chasm that separates church from synagogue. We have come to accept as permanent an alienation that Paul would not and did not accept.

Because of this, gentile readers have differing responses to chaps. 8 and 9; we cherish chap. 8 because it speaks of God's love for *us*, but we pass over chap. 9 because it speaks of God's love for someone else. We are not disturbed by the possibility that his love may in fact have let them go, though we rely on the promise that he will not let us go. We assume that Jews belong to another religion, having forfeited their right to God's care. Such attitudes make us as ethnocentric as were Paul's Jewish enemies.

The study of 9:1–5 calls us to remember the situation Paul faced. Jesus, the other apostles, Paul, and most Christians were Jews, a tiny Jewish minority subject to the hostility of the Jewish majority. Chap. 8 assured this minority, "regarded as sheep to be slaughtered," that God loved them. Their distress could not separate them from God's love because that distress bound them to Jesus who also had been killed by his kinsmen. But that same distress required on their part a love for their persecutors similar to Jesus' love for them. As a follower of Jesus, Paul could see no alternative for himself but to love his enemies. That is why his wish in 9:3 could never be granted. Love for his brothers could never result in being cut off from Christ; only hatred would have had that result.

In reading 9:1–5, therefore, we must recognize how far away the church has moved from Paul. In many centuries and many countries we have a record of treating the synagogue with all the indignities mentioned in 8:35–36. We do not bless God for his gifts to Israel (as in 9:4), but rather assume that those gifts have ceased. We praise the apostle verbally but repudiate his position. This lesson raises the question: In what concrete ways can we today share Paul's sorrow (v. 2), his wish (v. 3), his confession of indebtedness, and his gratitude to God (v. 4)?

Gospel: Matt. 14:22–33. Most readers, when they read this colorful story, visualize a scene during the lifetime of Jesus. That is entirely legitimate, even though it raises endless difficulties when the story is taken as bare-bones journalism. We should, however, also try to visualize a somewhat different scene. Imagine a situation about the year A.D. 85, perhaps in ancient Syria, in which a Christian teacher was addressing a church composed mainly of Jews who were subject, like Paul, to great hostility from their kinsmen. In this church the leaders are trying to provide the same kind of courageous leadership that had earlier been given by the apostles, many of whom had been martyred (like Peter). How would this story *read* in that church?

The readers would have had special empathy for the preceding story of the wilderness banquet. They would surely have sensed many subtle connections between that banquet and their own Eucharist, and to the table spread by the Lord in the presence of enemies (Ps. 23). Leaders would have been led to confess that, like their predecessors, they were unable to feed the crowds apart from Jesus' own help. The account of the sudden hurricane on the lake would have held special interest for these leaders. The time: the darkest section of the night, three hours before dawn, when the powers of darkness are greatest and human hearts are most apprehensive. The place: in a small boat far from land where sailors are most at the mercy of wind and waves. (Should one recall the darkness on the face of the waters in the story of creation [Gen. 1:2]?) The danger: the very ferocity of the storm had made these men keenly aware of the absence of Jesus. Their own "authority" seemed wholly inadequate in proportion to the forces arrayed against them (apathy, scorn, ostracism, mob violence, official trials). They feared not only for their own lives but for the success of their mission (compare Elijah fleeing to Horeb!). Only Jesus could counter their weakness and despair. The story tells of Jesus' ability to come to them at the point of their greatest emergency and to exert his authority over their enemies. (Read successive verses of the hymn "How Firm a Foundation.")

If we can visualize these church leaders in Syria, we can discern special nuances in the episode of Peter's efforts to overcome the same wind and waves. His walking on the water symbolizes his immunity to despair so long as he trusted his Lord; his sinking demonstrates vividly how that immunity is destroyed by doubting the Lord's presence in the storm. It may be that leaders in the church can be saved only by Jesus' stern rebuke (not unlike God's rebuke of Elijah). The rebuke itself proves who it is who is still in control of the situation, the same person who has sent his servants on a hazardous mission.

HOMILETICAL INTERPRETATION

First Lesson: 1 Kings 19:9–18. When difficulties arise and danger threatens, we find it easy to respond as Elijah did. We have struggled valiantly to accomplish some worthwhile goal, and things have gone wrong so that the whole project is lost. We have been subject to the ridicule of those who obviously do not understand who we are and what we are trying to do. In such circumstances we too may want to run away, to feel sorry for ourselves, to give it all up.

There is no doubt that Elijah was facing a tough situation. He had bested the prophets of Baal, but then Jezebel had vowed to see to it that Elijah was killed. So Elijah fled, and sat down under a broom tree and lamented: "It is enough; now, O Lord, take away my life; for I am no better than my fathers." Then he went on to Horeb where God met him and asked what he was doing there, and again Elijah lamented: "I have been very jealous for the Lord, the God of hosts; for the people of Israel have forsaken thy covenant, thrown down thy altars, and slain thy prophets with the sword; and I, even I only, am left; and they seek my life, to take it away."

Now God did not exactly sit down and tell Elijah how much he sympathized with him, and agree with him that things were really tough when no one would support him, and commiserate with him in his sense of being alone and rejected. God had another word for Elijah: Get back to work. He sent him back to anoint kings over Syria and Israel, and to anoint Elisha as the prophet to succeed him. In effect God told Elijah not to feel so sorry for himself at being all alone, because he was not alone. There were still the faithful in Israel, seven thousand who had not bowed to Baal. When despair and self-pity threaten to turn us in on ourselves, God turns us out from ourselves to the tasks still undone and declares to us that we are never as alone as we sometimes like to think.

Second Lesson: Rom. 9:1–5. Paul had significant differences with his fellow Jews, differences which brought personal suffering, threat, and anguish to Paul. The differences reveal the depth of his commitment to Jesus Christ and the sensitivity of his understanding of what faithfulness to Christ means. Four aspects of Paul's relationship with the Jews can be discerned in the passage from Romans.

First, Paul really cared for the Jews who harrassed him and fought him. In as solemn a fashion as possible Paul declared that he had "great sorrow and unceasing anguish" in his heart. In struggles with others, and especially when pushed to the point of despair by them, we may develop deep animosities, but Paul was able to keep his genuine concern for the Jews and cried out in anguish for them.

Second, Paul was willing to sacrifice himself for them. "For I could wish that I myself were accursed and cut off from Christ for the sake of my brethren, my kinsmen by race." Paul did suffer, and it was for the sake of those he was seeking to reach with the good news of God's love for them as it had been given in Jesus Christ.

Third, he appreciated what the Jews had to offer. "They are Israelites, and to them belong the sonship, the glory, the covenants, the giving of the law, the worship, and the promises; to them belong the patriarchs, and of their race, according to the flesh, is the Christ." In dealing with those with whom we differ seriously, whether the differences be political or economic or social or religious, we need to be mindful of the gifts which they have to offer to us and to others.

Finally, Paul saw the Jews as people of God. "God who is over all be blessed forever. Amen." No matter what the provocation, we dare not look at others as though they were outside the care and concern of God. There are difficult times in dealing with others, but Paul's deep passion for those who made life hard for him, serves as witness of the way in which Christ enables us to deal creatively with those hard relationships.

Gospel: Matt. 14:22–33. The disciples of Jesus found themselves in a desperate moment. As the exegetical comment points out, the story of the disciples floundering in a boat in a storm in the middle of the night is one with which the early church could readily identify, and one which relates to times we have known. When Jesus came to them, Peter ventured out of the boat to go to the Lord. He stayed afloat until he began to fear and doubt. Then, as he was sinking, he cried out: "Lord, save me." Peter's cry is a fitting and effective plea in moments of desperation. It was a cry uttered in anguish. It was a cry forced from his lips in a moment of fear and doubt. It was a cry which brought the word of rebuke from Jesus for his faithlessness. But it was a cry to which Jesus responded.

Each of the texts reports on the coming of God to people under pressure. When Elijah had to flee for his life, he headed toward Horeb, the mount of God. As he lay in the wilderness on the way there, an angel ministered to him. When he got to Horeb the Lord came to him. When he stood before the mount, the Lord came to him "in a still small voice." When Elijah was in the depths of his despair and ran away in fear and thought that he wanted to die, God cared for him. Before the mount he was able to discern the voice of God rebuking him for his self-pity, but setting him on the way out of his despair. For those who seek the mount of the Lord and those who have the sensitivity to hear, there is the promise in this story that God comes "in a still small voice."

Paul also dealt with his difficult situation in relation to the Jews in the confidence that God was sustaining and supporting him. "I am speaking the truth in Christ, I am not lying; my conscience bears me witness in the Holy Spirit." Inner conviction that we are right is no guarantee that we have a hold on the truth. But as we seek to discern the truth in Christ, God's Spirit is at work enabling us to bear witness.

Finally, for the disciples and for Peter, the love and power of God came to them in Jesus Christ. It was Christ whom they saw coming to them in the midst of the storm. It was Christ who reached out to Peter when he cried in desperation, "Lord, save me."

The Thirteenth Sunday after Pentecost

Lutheran	Roman Catholic	Episcopal	Pres/UCC/Chr	Meth/COCU
Isa. 56:1, 6–8	Isa. 56:1, 6–7	Isa. 56:1 (2–5), 6–7	Isa. 56:1–7	Isa. 56:1–8
Rom. 11:13–15, 29–32	Rom. 11:13–15, 29–32	Rom. 11:13–15, 29–32	Rom. 11:13–16, 29–32	Rom. 11:13–16, 29–32
Matt. 15:21–28	Matt. 15:21–28	Matt. 15:21–28	Matt. 15:21–28	Matt. 15:21–28

EXEGESIS

First Lesson: Isa. 56:1–8. The Book of Isaiah was accepted as sacred Scripture, as the word of God, both by Jesus and his followers on one side and by his scribal and Pharisaic opponents on the other. It was far from accidental that many controversies between these two groups centered on interpretations of Isaiah. Two of these controversies in particular were fueled by two different ways of reading this text.

In one instance Jesus quoted Isa. 56:7 in his attack upon the rulers of the temple (Mark 11:15–19; John 2:13–22). God has intended the temple as a house of prayer for all peoples, including outcasts, eunuchs, and foreigners. But the leaders had turned this place of prayer into an open market for their own profit. It is not surprising that they defended themselves against this guerrilla attack; almost certainly this controversy was a factor in the death of Jesus.

In the other instance, all the Gospels report the running battles between Jesus and the Pharisees over correct ways to observe the Sabbath. They attacked him as one who repeatedly profaned this holy day, made holy by God's own decree. (Modern Seventh-Day Adventists and Seventh-Day Baptists may remind us of how important the ancient Pharisees considered this command of God.) They were entirely sincere in accusing Jesus (along with Christians in Paul's and Matthew's churches) of defying the law of God. Again the evidence is overwhelming that this issue contributed to the death of Jesus. So when we try to interpret this text, we are immediately involved in agelong and bitter disputes. The text prompts many questions to which we should not expect unanimous answers.

For example, when we begin with Isaiah's statement concerning the temple and Jesus' interpretation of it, we may well ask how any religion can make its holy place a house of prayer for all nations, including its nonmembers and even its outcasts? Does not every religious institution become an institution by drawing boundaries that exclude some people? In other words, can Jesus' interpretation of Isaiah become standard practice?

The second series of questions is even more tricky. How does one determine that a person is profaning the Sabbath? Should we use the same tests the Pharisees applied to Jesus? Or did Jesus show by his justice and righteousness (Isa. 56:1) how a person truly keeps the Sabbath holy? The text reminds us that the conflicts of Isaiah's day have persisted through the centuries to our own day. A dilemma seems to be built into that text: Insistence on any such law as that of Sabbath observance will have the effect of excluding some people from temple worship.

Second Lesson: Rom. 11:13–15, 29–32. The art of exegesis is in large part the disciplined ability to see through the eyes of an ancient author and his audience, and to imagine how they viewed the world. In dealing with Romans, this means that a person must reconstruct the outlook of Christian congregations in Rome, some of which were largely Jewish in membership, and others which were largely Gentile (some of their debates are mirrored in 14:1—15:13). We must try to share the inherited attitudes of Jews toward Gentiles and of Gentiles toward Jews.

Imagine yourself a member of a house church made up of Jews. You would feel deeply that loyalty to God required strong precautions to avoid contamination by gentile contacts. You would feel that by their immoralities and blasphemies Gentiles had proven themselves incapa-

ble of holding to any covenant with God (Rom. 1:18–32). You would fear
the potential long-term results of converting Gentiles to Christ unless
they promised to observe the same holy days and to avoid unclean foods
(Rom. 14:5–6). You would oppose any apostle who accepted gentile
converts without demanding such promises, since he would be under-
mining the boundaries between God's people and paganism.

But now suppose yourself a member of a gentile commune, sharing
their inherited attitudes toward Jews. You would no doubt resent their
claims to holiness and superiority in the eyes of God. You would welcome other Gentiles as members without stipulating that they be cir-
cumcised, observe the Sabbath, and eat only kosher food. You would
have little interest in making converts from Judaism, but rather insist on
complete separation of the church from the synagogue.

In chap. 9 Paul wrote primarily for the first group, the Jewish believers. In 11:13 he turns to the Gentiles, speaking as their apostle who has
magnified his ministry to them at the cost of ostracism from his own
people. He makes five important points.

1. They should not think of the branches of the olive tree as holy
(whether Jew or Gentile), but should locate holiness only in the root on
which all the branches depend.

2. Contrary to popular opinions, Paul's own efforts to convert Gentiles have actually been motivated by his desire to save Jews; he has
followed the way of dealing with Israel which God and Christ had
chosen.

3. Faith in the resurrection of Christ is demonstrated most decisively
when those who at first reject the gospel are transformed into believers
(v. 15).

4. Both groups have been disobedient and guilty of rejecting God's
call, so both have been recipients of mercy in that very disobedience
and guilt.

5. Though his own people have become enemies, God loves them
(v. 28) and will never revoke the gifts he has given them.

Roman Christians found it difficult to understand and to accept those
points; modern American Christians no less so.

Gospel: Matt. 15:21–28. All three lessons this week deal with outcasts: in Isaiah with eunuchs and foreigners, in Romans with gentile
antagonism toward Jews, and in Matthew with Jewish suspicions of
Gentiles. As we have noted, Matthew addressed his Gospel to churches
in Syria, most of which were Jewish in membership. This anecdote is
pungent with typical Jewish antipathies toward a gentile mother and her

daughter, living in pagan territory outside the Holy Land. The story recognizes some of the arguments used to support those antipathies. Yes, Jesus had limited his ministry to "the lost sheep of the house of Israel." Some Syrian Christians may have insisted on following that example. Matthew also admits that Jesus had ordered his co-workers in 10:6: "Go nowhere among the Gentiles." Some of his readers were appealing to that precedent.

Although the Evangelist recognizes the force of these arguments, he refuses to draw the same inferences. He suggests the significance of Jesus' journey into a gentile region after he had denied that Gentiles are by nature unclean (15:7–20). In that region he had tested the faith of the mother and had been amazed at the strength of that faith. He had in fact chosen to heal the Canaanite daughter, thus extending the boundaries of the kingdom to include her. As a result of this act of mercy, many people from that region (that is, many Gentiles) had come to glorify the God of Israel (v. 31). Such episodes prepared the readers of Matthew for the climax of the story. When the risen Lord appeared to the eleven disciples he explicitly commanded them to widen the range of their mission to include all nations, and the Greek word for nations could as well be translated: Gentiles (28:19).

It may be that in his very next story in Matthew 15 the Evangelist was making the same point. This second instance of Jesus feeding a multitude may have been designed to suggest a gentile Eucharist. In the first wilderness meal, the twelve baskets of fragments may have symbolized food adequate for the twelve tribes of Israel; in this second miracle, the seven baskets may have symbolized food adequate for all nations. That is a possible reading, though by no means a definitive one.

HOMILETICAL INTERPRETATION

All three texts for this week deal with the issues raised when some in-group is identified and separated from others. All three texts reflect the tension between the positive gains made by such identification and the problems raised when persons are separated from each other as "ins" and "outs." The texts deal with situations in which the in-group identification is based at least partly on the religious faith of the people involved. Because religion deals with the fundamental values and perceptions of persons, the tensions between the insiders and the outsiders tend to be particularly difficult to deal with.

First Lesson: Isa. 56:1–8. The exegesis indicates the way in which the different interpretations of this text by Jesus and the Pharisees exacerbated the tensions between them and contributed to the opposition which led to the death of Jesus. Even ways of worship and keeping the Sabbath can divide people from one another, not only then but also today. There has recently been lively debate in a number of states over the blue laws which prohibit some kinds of stores or businesses from working on Sunday; the effort to legislate rules of the Sabbath leads to many ambiguities. Some kinds of stores can be open; some kinds of goods can be sold; some kinds of services can be rendered. Drawing the line between the permissible and the forbidden becomes extraordinarily difficult to do with consistency and fairness, and imposes standards on those who do not share in the conviction about the importance of the Sabbath.

Coming through the prophetic text there is a clear word about the importance of keeping the Sabbath, and a firm promise of the blessing which comes to those who do. The text does not tell us precisely what needs to be done in order to keep the Sabbath properly. But the word about the importance of the Sabbath does have something to say about the way in which people identify some as being part of their own group and others as being outsiders, for the text talks about the foreigners and about the eunuchs, who were indeed looked upon as outcasts. The lines were drawn between "us" and "them."

To those who are outcast or who feel themselves outcast on those grounds, the prophet speaks a strong word of inclusion as part of God's people. In keeping the Sabbath the eunuchs will know that in spite of having no issue to carry on their names they have an everlasting name before God. In keeping the Sabbath the foreigners will know that they are welcome in the house which "shall be called a house of prayer for all peoples." Israel may call some outcasts, but the Lord God "gathers the outcasts of Israel."

Second Lesson: Rom. 11:13–15, 29–32. A frequently articulated position holds that religious differences should not divide people because everyone is trying to get to the same place and all religions are equally helpful in accomplishing that goal. It seems certain that the apostle Paul would disagree violently with that view. With all the vigor which he possessed, Paul presented the claims of Christ. Certainly from the point of view of the Jews, Paul was a divisive influence and a troublemaker.

As Paul writes explicitly to the Gentiles in his letter to the Romans, he deals directly with the issue of the separation between themselves and the Jews. Although Paul has to hold convictions which exacerbate the divisions and the tensions, he never loses his deep concern for those who do not agree with him. He is never content simply to establish the superiority of his own view and group. He is not willing to leave his opponents in their plight. He wants the Jew to find the blessing of God which he has found in Christ.

The ways in which Paul sees the tension between Jew and Gentile, and his own role in relation to that tension, are instructive as we consider how to deal with those who differ with us.

First, Paul works in the hope and even the expectation that what apparently divides him from others can be in fact a means of reconciliation with them. He will not compromise, but believes that even the jealousy with which the Jews view his work can be a means of enabling them to see the truth. Second, Paul does not lodge all righteousness in himself and his own views. It is "the root" that is holy, and whatever holiness he has comes from that goodness of God on which he and all others depend. Furthermore, "God has consigned all men to disobedience, that he may have mercy upon all." In identifying our in-group against their out-group, we cannot claim that we are perfectly righteous while they are unrighteous. Both they and we are under the mercy of God. Third, Paul does not push any people beyond the claim and care of God. On the contrary, he affirms that though the present actions of the Jews may be in opposition to the gospel, "as regards his election they are beloved for the sake of their forefathers." Even those with whom we differ most sharply are within the care of God, and we must deal with them knowing that we ourselves have been forgiven and loved by God whatever we have done.

Gospel: Matt. 15:21–28. The behavior of Jesus as described in this incident surprises and puzzles us. Why would he speak those brutal words: "It is not fair to take the children's bread and throw it to the dogs." The foreign woman was an outsider. Jesus dealt with her as one.

What are we to make of this incident? First, Jesus' primary ministry *was* to his own people. He focused his attention on this people in this place at this time. He did not try to cover the whole world, but ministered in depth to those with whom he had a primary relationship. It is folly for us also to be so concerned with far places and other peoples that we miss the opportunity to minister to those who are closest to us.

Second, Jesus *did* heal the daughter of the woman. When the strength of her faith became evident, he reached out beyond the immediate circle of his people and responded to her plea. The blessing of God reaches out to all. While we may be called to focus our attention on the particular place where we are, we cannot cut off concern for those beyond that primary responsibility.

Finally, we may note what it means to be surprised by the behavior of Jesus in this incident. It means that we do find it out of character for Jesus, because we have learned through him that he came to bring the truth and grace of God to every person. We have learned through him that God cares for all of his children, and that he pushes us toward a sense of our oneness with all persons.

The Fourteenth Sunday after Pentecost

Lutheran	Roman Catholic	Episcopal	Pres/UCC/Chr	Meth/COCU
Exod. 6:2–8	Isa. 22:15, 19–23	Isa. 51:1–6	Isa. 22:19–23	Isa. 22:19–23
Rom. 11:33–36	Rom. 11:33–36	Rom. 11:33–36	Rom. 11:33–36	Rom. 11:33–36
Matt. 16:13–20	Matt. 16:13–20	Matt. 16:13–20	Matt. 16:13–20	Matt. 16:13–20

EXEGESIS

First Lesson: Isa. 22:19–23. In this passage Isaiah directed a prophecy against a steward, Shebna. From the prophecy we may learn much concerning the symbolic language used to describe sin and its punishment. Above all else Shebna desired fame and security. This is symbolized by his efforts to carve out of living rock a magnificent burial vault as a memorial to himself. A number of such memorials may still be seen in the Kidron valley near Jerusalem (cf. Matt. 23:27f.). The prophet describes various penalties for this presumption. God will play with Shebna like a boy playing with a yo-yo (vv. 17–18). He will displace the steward from his office by clothing another with the symbol of office, a robe. The belt, symbol of authority, will be placed around a successor's waist. In the successor's hand will be placed the rod or mace that betokens sovereign power. People will respect the successor as a father, and will rely on him for their survival. Like a peg driven firmly into the wall of a stone house, his family will hang on him their most precious possessions. He will be given charge of the keys so that he can include or exclude whomever he wills from the household of David. No human office is so famous or secure that it becomes immune to God's action.

Many of these symbols were used in the NT to describe the honor and authority that God had vested in Jesus (in Rev. 1:12–18, for example, one notes the robe, the belt, the rod, and the keys). Some of these symbols were used to describe the trust that Jesus invested in his own lieutenants (Matt. 16:13–20; 18:15–30). In fact, all faithful believers in Christ are visualized as wearing white robes, a mark of their office and authority. If one supposes that such symbols have lost their vitality, he needs only think of the inauguration of a president or the coronation of a Pope. It is at such times that we realize how much a community does need such a peg in its house, and how temporary such pegs are.

Second Lesson: Rom. 11:33–36. Few leaders of the church have shown more clearly the marks of greatness than has Paul, and few have been accorded greater reverence. As for Paul himself, it was his weakness and his lack of "impressive leadership credentials" that he could never forget (1 Cor. 2:1f.). This awareness of his own incompetence was in part a reaction to the overwhelming task that had been assigned to him: to work toward the salvation of "the full number" of Gentiles and of "all Israel" (11:25f.). This required the reconciliation to each other of these two segments of humankind, which had been at war for centuries. It was this mission that exposed him to hatred from both segments. Jews, including many Christians in Rome, looked upon him as a traitor; Gentiles, including many in Roman churches, rejected him as a Jew and as an Israel-lover (9:1–5). The more he succeeded in his task, the more these antagonisms flourished, vivid evidence of the egocentricity of both groups.

Paul was of course baffled by their failure to understand him, but even more alarmed by their misreading of the gospel. That alarm may be detected in today's text. Both claimed that their own prejudices represented the mind of the Lord. Both visualized themselves as God's counselors, fully qualified to advise God on how to handle their opponents. Both believed that God owed them a special reward for their defense of his interests. In Paul's mind the three rhetorical questions of vv. 34–35 called for negative answers, but in fact Roman Christians had been giving positive answers, thus rejecting the truth of Isaiah's insight (Isa. 40:13) and forgetting God's rebuke of self-justifying Job (Job 41:11). They supposed that God's ways and judgments were entirely "searchable" and "scrutable" because God's thoughts in effect coincided with their own.

The apostle, however, was not content with the biting sarcasm of these questions; he proceeded to make several positive declarations about the core features of the gospel. In v. 33a we find an explosive exclamation concerning God's amazing mercy for both Jews and Gentiles. God could even deal with the self-centered prejudices of Paul's Christian adversaries. Their conception of the wealth of God was indeed very shallow, but that shallowness disclosed all the more clearly the depth of God's love. However, in the end Paul relied not on arguments but on a traditional doxology, which his readers in the Roman churches had no doubt used in their worship. He relied on that doxology to suggest to these quarreling Christians the degree to which they had been claiming glory for themselves. As for Paul himself, the doxology meant that he included even his failures in Rome to be embraced by the prepositions *from, through,* and *to.*

Gospel: Matt. 16:13–20. Since the Reformation, this story, a Matthean expansion of the Marcan narrative (Mark 8:27–30), has been a battleground between Roman Catholics and Protestants. It has been combined with the postbiblical doctrine of episcopal succession to establish a doctrine of papal authority that constitutes a major obstacle to ecumenical advance. The association of this text with the other texts for this Sunday is suggestive. To what extent is the gift of keys to Peter linked to their removal from Shebna in Isaiah 22? To what extent do Paul's arguments in Romans 11 provide correction to the pretensions that so frequently accompany ecclesiastical office?

The central accent of the original story falls on the identity of Jesus as Messiah and Son of God. Because of Peter's correct answer in v. 16, Jesus gives him a new name, the Greek *petros* which is so near the Greek word for rock, *petra,* that Peter becomes the rock on which Jesus will build his church. Jesus promises that this church will overcome the gates of Hades, the source of all the demonic powers that resist God's plans. With the keys Jesus gives to this *rock* the authority to control access to the kingdom of heaven.

Other passages in Matthew suggest that the reader, in thinking about this story, should remember three points. First, the promise of the keys to Peter as an individual should be taken in conjunction with Matt. 18:15–20, where binding and loosing are viewed as a "collegial" responsibility. Second, the praise of Peter for his openness to divine revelation (v. 17) should be balanced with the condemnation of Peter for his surrender to satanic wiles (vv. 22–23) and for his misunderstanding of Jesus (17:5). Third, Jesus immediately linked the verbal confession of faith in him with the necessity of surrendering one's life for his sake

(vv. 24f.). Along with John (John 21), Matthew recognized that Peter's confession would in the end be made fully authentic by his martyrdom. How does this apply to Catholic-Protestant debates over papal primacy? At least we may say that the logic of Paul's rebuke to Jews and Gentiles in Rom. 11:33–36 applies with equal force to these two modern groups of Christians. By joining Paul in his doxology, all Christians may find a common ground for discussing their divergent interpretations of Matthew 16.

HOMILETICAL INTERPRETATION

In his story, *S.S. San Pedro,* James Gould Cozzens describes the journey of an ill-fated ship from Hoboken, New Jersey to Argentina. Captain Clendening is in command of the ship, a man of long experience at sea, but a man now ill and in constant pain. A couple of days out of Hoboken a heavy storm hits, and the ship suffers extensive damage. The captain fails to respond. He waits too long to change course and speed. He does not move aggressively to have the damage repaired. When it becomes clear that the ship may founder, he hesitates to give the order to get passengers and crew into the lifeboats. He is the captain and no one else can give the crucial orders; he is the captain but he fails to exercise the authority which is his. The ship founders and sinks and most of the people on board drown.

This story gives dramatic illustration of the crucial role of authority in human affairs. Persons must be vested with the responsibility of making decisions. The health of a community and even the survival of persons is dependent upon the exercising of that authority. Isaiah describes the way in which Eliakim is invested with authority. Certain symbols are given to him. He is to become as "a father to the inhabitants of Jerusalem and to the house of Judah." In a different image he is described as a peg fixed in a sure place. The passage from Matthew also describes a person being invested with authority. Jesus hears the affirmation of Peter that He is the Christ, and then declares that Peter has the keys to the kingdom of heaven.

Even if authority in human affairs is ordained by God, it is evident that the authority is not always exercised in accordance with his will. The verses from Isaiah in the First Lesson deal with the symbols and reality of the power given to Eliakim. The verses just preceding and just following the text indicate some of the temptations and corruption of authority. Eliakim was given authority because his predecessor,

Shebna, had misused his power. He had hewn a tomb for himself (v. 16). It was a mark of status to have a big tomb, and Shebna had used the common resources to create a monument to himself. There is also mention of the splendid chariots which he demanded for his own use. The judgment of God fell on Shebna because he had used his position for self-aggrandizement and for personal luxuries.

The verses immediately following the text indicate that Eliakim did not fare much better in his exercise of the authority entrusted to him. He was called "a peg in a sure place," but the story goes on to talk about the day when "the peg that was fastened in a sure place will give way" (v. 25).

As the exegesis of the passage from Matthew makes clear, the granting of the keys of the kingdom of heaven by Jesus has not solved the problems of authority in the Christian community. Claims of authority have been made which have divided and continue to divide the church. As in any human institution, power within the church can be used corruptly for personal gain or institutional dominance. Claiming to have the powers of the keys to the kingdom of heaven may tempt the church to coerce persons to give their support.

Granted that there are always temptations related to the exercise of authority, and granted that every human being will know the corruption of power, there are still ways in which persons can exercise rightfully the authority given to them. All these texts suggest ways in which persons can be helped to deal rightly with whatever powers they possess.

First, all power is to be exercised as accountable before God. It was God who gave Eliakim the symbols and the reality of the power which he had. It was God who took away the authority of Shebna when he abused the trust which had been given to him. Power is not something given to persons to do with as they please. One way to use power rightly is to seek to be faithful to God in the decisions which are made.

Second, the person in authority must use that power for the welfare of those who are affected by the decisions made. When the prophet was still hopeful about Eliakim he described him as one who would be "a father to the inhabitants of Jerusalem and to the house of Judah." He would care for the people under him.

Third, authority should be exercised with vivid awareness of human limitation. Decisions have to be made, and people have to make them using the best information they have and making the best judgments they can. But the judgments of human beings are never to be confused with the judgments of God. Paul was struggling with two communities, each of which thought that it had the truth of God. Paul sees more clearly. He is convinced that the answer is, "No one." when he asks: "For who has known the mind of the Lord or who has been his counselor?" When persons in authority are tempted to believe that they have all the answers, that their judgment is beyond question, that by virtue of their position they speak with the authority of God, they need to recall Paul's words about the ways of God: "How unsearchable are his judgments and how inscrutable are his ways!"

Finally, authority is better exercised by one in the role of a servant rather than by one in the role of a master. The notions of authority and servanthood are frequently not related. The one in authority is the one who does *not* have to be a servant, the one who can demand that others are the servants. But after Jesus had talked about giving to Peter the keys of the kingdom of heaven, he immediately described the way in which he would suffer many things from the authorities in Jerusalem. Surely those who have the keys of the kingdom of heaven are not called to exalt themselves, but rather are called to minister to those who God claims for his kingdom.

The Fifteenth Sunday after Pentecost

Lutheran	Roman Catholic	Episcopal	Pres/UCC/Chr	Meth/COCU
Jer. 15:15–21	Jer. 20:7–9	Jer. 15:15–21	Jer. 20:7–9	Jer. 15:15–21
Rom. 12:1–8	Rom. 12:1–2	Rom. 12:1–8	Rom. 12:1–7	Rom. 12:1–8
Matt. 16:21–26	Matt. 16:21–27	Matt. 16:21–27	Matt. 16:21–28	Matt. 16:21–28

EXEGESIS

First Lesson: Jer. 15:15–21. Few passages so vividly portray the inner turmoil of a prophet whose vocation under God and whose love for his people makes him the object of their ridicule and rejection. This situation prompted in him a bitter debate with the God who had ordered him to prophesy to his people. How could words which in themselves were a joy (v. 16) produce such agony? Had God become "a deceitful brook" which, after being flooded with the spring runoff, had dried up with summer's drought? It may well be that only a person who has shared such agony of heart can fully grasp Jeremiah's words. In his struggle with God, punctuated by pained *why's* (vv. 15–18) and by God's answers (vv. 19–21), Jeremiah was kin to Paul in his inner torment in Romans 9—11 and to the Messiah in his agony in Gethsemane (Mark 14).

What kind of exegesis is demanded by a text like this? A reconstruction of the political and economic situation in Jeremiah's day would help, but not much. We could try to find the exact date and place of Jeremiah's protest, but those facts would be quite irrelevant. What is needed is poetic insight, for this is exquisite, if also pain-charged poetry. Why did this prophet consider his wound incurable (v. 18)? He had discovered that his vocation of eating and speaking God's words had unleashed a torrent of public abuse. He could, of course, escape the abuse by repudiating the vocation. In a sense God was the cause of his perplexity; that is why he took his case back to God. No wonder he asked, *why*?

An interpreter must have enough empathy to understand that *why*, but also enough to grasp God's reassurance. To be sure, God does not take steps to reduce the agony or to heal the wound. He simply promises the prophet that if he utters "what is precious" the public that fights against him will not prevail over him. He will become a fortified wall of bronze. One may well ask what kind of victory this is. Is it simply another way of saying, "One man with God is in the majority" or is there an inner victory much more convincing than the truth expressed by that pious cliché?

Second Lesson: Rom. 12:1–8. We should remember that throughout Romans Paul was trying to reconcile the divisions among believers. As a Jewish apostle who sought to convert Gentiles, he had helped to accentuate those divisions. Jewish believers must have said: "How can he expect us to welcome Gentiles into the close fellowship of Israel?" Their gentile counterparts must have said: "How can he expect us to welcome those Jewish believers who have challenged our right to belong?"

When we keep that cluster of animosities in mind, as well as the debates embedded in chaps. 9—11, the collection of exhortations in chap. 12 take on new meanings. The *therefore* in 12:1 indicates a strong link to the preceding arguments. It is because of the depth of God's mercies (11:33f.) that Paul can make his appeal simultaneously to both camps, for both had received those mercies. When in the same verse

Paul says *brethren*, he probably intended to include members of both camps, many of whom refused to call Paul himself by that intimate term. The appeal to present themselves as living sacrifices surely included the kind of self-denial that is expressed in considering those others (whether Gentiles or Jews) as better than themselves. Only a genuine renewal of the mind could enable them to jettison the egoism and pride by which they were still conformed to this world (v. 2). So each of the injunctions in this catechetical summary of virtues was relevant to both sides in Rome at the point of their deepest divisions.

This series of teachings offers a sample of the form of catechetical instruction provided in many early congregations. It may be that each convert was expected to memorize such a collection, for instant recall in dealing with one problem after another. Each command is general, inclusive, unqualified, universal, simple to memorize, and relevant to many emergencies. Yet, at the same time, each command is crystal clear and entirely specific. Paul undoubtedly found many occasions where he needed to appeal to these ethical basics. The appearance of this collection in Romans is an excellent example of how generalized principles could be brought to bear on immediate problems, a sample of how the best "situation ethics" can be grounded in eternal ethical verities.

Gospel: Matt. 16:21–26. A key term in this passage is the Greek *skandalon* for which the RSV has adopted the English *hindrance* (v. 23b), a word much weaker than the original. The RSV has in the margin a more accurate *stumbling-block*. The Greek term is so central to the Gospel that to misread this metaphor can be disastrous. The image is of two persons, one of whom is walking on a path to reach a particular goal when the other places in his path a rock or snare that causes the first to stumble and to fall, putting that person's goal out of reach. Modern warfare has created a similar metaphor in the term "booby trap." In NT language, this "stone of stumbling" either prevents a person from believing or it causes him to lose his faith, and thereby his salvation.

Early Christians found the crucifixion of Christ to be both a *skandalon* and a necessary part of God's plan (1 Cor. 1:23). As Messiah, Jesus recognized that this stone had actually been placed in his path by God (1 Pet. 2:4–8), not to make him stumble but to qualify him as Savior. It was reaction to the same stone which separated believers from unbelievers. Such is the background for the episode in Matthew. When Jesus spoke of the necessity of the cross, Peter objected and urged Jesus to take another path, which would in fact have ended his power to save.

Jesus recognized Peter's protest as a maneuver on the part of Satan, and he rebuked his chief disciple in the strongest possible language. Since the apostle was, in this, spokesman for the devil, Jesus had to address Peter and the devil simultaneously. If Jesus had agreed with Peter he would have forfeited his mission. So on this occasion Jesus did not stumble, but Peter did; his earlier confession of fear (Matt. 14:29–32) made the absence of faith all the more culpable.

It was more, though, than an absence of faith. Peter's refusal to accept the cross for Jesus meant also Peter's refusal to accept his own vocation. For Jesus had made it clear that every disciple faced the same prospect as his own: a suffering for others that would lead to brutal martyrdom (vv. 24–26). Peter's protest effectively closed that path for him, at least for the time being. The path was still closed in Matt. 26:30–56. When the shepherd was struck down, all the sheep were scattered (or were caused to stumble) by the shepherd's death. As on the earlier occasion, Peter was again blind to the danger. Matthew saw the story of Peter's fall as among the most terrible stories in the Gospel.

Even that fall on the part of Peter would not be the last *skandalon*. According to Matt. 16:24–26, Jesus knew that the later requirements of apostleship would become a new booby trap. He warned them that after his own death they would face their own equivalent of Gethsemane and Calvary. Satan would again tempt them. Almost certainly Matthew saw the same cross (v. 24) as a continuing *skandalon* for members of his own churches.

HOMILETICAL INTERPRETATION

When people are faithful to the call of God, their lives seem to become complex and tumultuous rather than simple and peaceful. The texts for this Sunday give striking demonstration that a peaceful and untroubled life is not the sure outcome for those who hear the call of God and respond with faith.

First Lesson: Jer. 15:15–21. Whereas the portrayal of an ideal person of faith in terms of all-pervasive calmness, serenity, and peace leaves us feeling unsatisfied and frustrated because we cannot be like that, the picture of Jeremiah may come close to the ambiguities of our lives and our efforts to be faithful. To be sure, we are not called to be prophets like Jeremiah, and most of us will never reach either the heights or the depths which marked his life. But we do glimpse in him something of the dynamic of God's relationship to persons. What we see in Jeremiah does relate to our own experiences of faith and doubt, of peace and turmoil, of certainty and confusion.

What kind of man is Jeremiah, this man of God? He is a man who knows despair and who can succumb to self-pity. In the verses just preceding those assigned for today, he laments, "Woe is me, my mother, that you bore me." He is a man who vacillates wildly in his dealings with his enemies. He beseeches God to "take vengeance for me on my persecutors," and yet in the preceding verses he talks of how he had entreated God for the good of his enemies and pleaded with God on their behalf.

In a lovely image he talks of eating the words of God. The words became a part of him and nourished his life. In that process the words of God became a joy and a delight to him. He knows himself to have been called by the name of the Lord and that too brought joy to him. On the other hand, he complains bitterly about what the Lord has brought upon him. Because he has tried to speak the Lord's word and be the Lord's witness, people have shunned him and he has not sat in the company of merrymakers. In a bitter moment he demands to know why there is no end to his pain and no healing for his wounds. With vehemence he wants to know if God is like a brook that fails just when the people are in desperate need of water. When our own relationship with God becomes difficult and uncertain, Jeremiah serves as an example of one who was forthright in declaring both the joy and the pain of that relationship.

After Jeremiah's hard words about God's failures, the Lord says to him: "If you return, I will restore you, and you shall stand before me. If you utter what is precious, and not what is worthless, you shall be as my mouth." God does not reject the prophet, but he does not leave him to wallow in his self-pity. God calls us to turn back to him and admonishes us to speak precious words rather than worthless words, true words rather than false ones. There is a final word to Jeremiah and to us, the word that whatever comes, God will be with us. "For I am with you to save you and deliver you, says the Lord."

Second Lesson: Rom. 12:1–8. In our society there is strong pressure on all of us to conform to the standards of the world around us. That pressure is felt in such relatively insignificant matters as fashions in dress and appearance: the length of skirts, the width of ties, the cut of hair. It is a pressure felt in terms of life style: the accepted ways of doing things, the kind of entertainment, the right clubs or groups. More significantly, it is a pressure to accept fundamental values: the goals which are sought, the ways in which other persons are treated, the standards of conduct.

In his letter to the Romans, Paul alerts his readers that faithful living must not be confused with being at ease in the ways of the world around us. Paul puts the situation not only in negative terms, "do not be conformed to this world," but also in positive terms, "be transformed by the renewal of your mind." The rest of the twelfth chapter of Romans works out something of what it means not to be conformed to this world but to be transformed. Do not be conformed to the world's delight in the symbols of power and prestige, but be transformed in the awareness that we "are one body in Christ." Do not be conformed to the world's willingness to exploit other persons for our own benefit, but "let love be genuine." Do not be conformed to the world's way of vengeance and hatred for our enemies, but "bless those who persecute you." Do not be conformed to the world's view that richness of life is to be equated with richness in things, but "be aglow with the Spirit, serve the Lord."

Gospel: Matt. 16:21–26. The church lives in a continual tension between its conviction that the good news is open to everyone, and its awareness that the Christian life sets stringent demands. So the church requires confirmation classes, expects a certain level of giving, and demands active participation in the program.

Such efforts of the church to set standards for membership may be helpful, but they are not to be equated with the radical demands of discipleship which Jesus laid upon Peter and the other disciples. Surely Jesus did not equate discipleship with a life of placid ease. Peter could not cope when Jesus talked of what he was going to suffer, for he had not grasped what being faithful to God might mean.

When Jesus set the demands for discipleship he did not talk in terms of rules to be followed or specific tasks to be accomplished. Rather, he talked about the need for persons to deny themselves. That does not mean self-denigration, but it does mean getting oneself out of the center, a hard move to make for all of us. He talked about the call for persons to take up the cross. In some generations that has been fulfilled literally. In all generations it has meant the willingness to take upon oneself in suffering and sacrifice the burdens of others. Finally, Jesus talked about following him. That is an open invitation, for we do not know exactly where he will lead us or what he will ask of us.

The Sixteenth Sunday after Pentecost

Lutheran	Roman Catholic	Episcopal	Pres/UCC/Chr	Meth/COCU
Ezek. 33:7–9	Ezek. 33:7–9	Ezek. 33:(1–6), 7–11	Ezek. 33:7–9	Ezek. 33:1–11
Rom. 13:1–10	Rom. 13:8–10	Rom. 12:9–21	Rom. 13:8–10	Rom. 12:9–13:10
Matt. 18:15–20	Matt. 18:15–20	Matt. 18:15–20	Matt. 18:15–20	Matt. 18:15–20

EXEGESIS

First Lesson: Ezek. 33:7–11. Through the early centuries of Israel's history, no one was more important than the prophet. Today's lesson reveals some of the distinctive features of that vocation. First of all, a prophet is a representative of the people whom the people have chosen from among themselves (33:2). Second, this representative is a person to whom the word of the Lord has come; God has chosen him to serve as a spokesman. Third, the prophet is charged with being a watchman who can warn the city against approaching disaster. Refusal to give warning in time, in accordance with God's word, makes the watchman guilty of the blood of his people. The responsibility of "blowing the trumpet" (alerting residents to an approaching army) was not taken lightly. Either to flee at the first sight of danger or to sound the alarm without good reason constituted a gross dereliction of duty.

Our lesson also illustrates biblical notions of how life is gained or lost. How one responds to the word of God through the watchman marks the difference between life and death. That response is a matter of *turning*. When listeners turn, they live; when they refuse to turn, they die. But death is never the only option, for it is always possible to turn back. Neither the watchman nor his hearers can claim an alibi for not turning; they can never charge their death to God's account. As he lives, he desires only life. So the measure of life is God's life. Those who suppose that life simply means continued existence on the earth have missed Ezekiel's message. To live is to turn toward God's life; to die is to refuse to turn. This attitude toward life and death reinforces the conception of the importance of the prophet's work, since everything hangs on the trustworthiness of the word from God. And ultimately all life depends upon that short phrase, "As I live." Nothing so clearly shows the uniqueness of biblical faith. To see the world through the eyes of Ezekiel is to find life where many find death, and to find death where many find life.

Second Lesson: Rom. 12:9–21. We have already noticed that the Christians in Rome formed a small minority that was subject to violent persecution by both pagan populace and public officials. Not more than a decade after this letter the emperor Nero would execute many Christians, perhaps including both Paul and Peter, as one of his reactions to the disastrous fire. Moreover, we have also noticed how the various Christian congregations were themselves bitterly divided, not only in their ways of meeting this public venom, but also by inherited Jewish-Gentile animosities. Each of the teachings in this familiar catalog of virtues takes on new meaning when the reader keeps these problems in mind.

We should notice, for example, the evidence for the existence of those vicious circles in which communities get trapped. Those who become impatient in tribulation (v. 12) often invite increasing impatience and added suffering. Those who refuse hospitality to fellow Christians (v. 13) are refused hospitality by them. When cursing prompts cursing (v. 14) the chain of recriminations continues unbroken. To laugh at the misfortunes of others (v. 15) guarantees mounting hostility. When evil is repaid by evil, when every injustice is met by the demand for vengeance, when a person or a congregation tries to overcome evil by evil, all those involved become "conformed to this world" (12:2), a world which lives by the laws of tit for tat. In such dilemmas it is essential for Christians to know the identity of their real enemy. Is it the person who does evil to me, or is it my ingrained inclination to defend my own rights? Is the real enemy "flesh and blood" or, as Paul wrote in Ephesians, is it the "world rulers of this present darkness" (Eph. 6:12)?

Each of the axioms of Christian behavior listed in our text aims to break some vicious circle by introducing action dictated by "the renewal of your mind" (Rom. 12:2). This is what happens when cursing is met by blessing, and pride is countered by humility. To feed an enemy not only breaks the expected pattern, it carries a message to that enemy about God. God can be trusted to execute vengeance. But something is even more important than that: God has himself established the pattern, the virtuous circle, of overcoming evil with good. That is why Christians can safely rejoice in hope and be "aglow with the Spirit" as they serve this Lord.

Gospel: Matt. 18:15–20. A Christian congregation is composed of members who try to follow the teachings of Romans 12. But it requires more than such efforts by its members; the congregation needs to develop judicial procedures for handling disciplinary problems in line with such teachings. The Gospel for the day reflects the early stages in the development of those judicial procedures. This evangelist was a church leader who took seriously his obligation to provide this guidance. In this guidance he tries above all to protect the member who is charged with deviant behavior.

First of all, the leaders of a congregation must respect the right to privacy on the part of the offender; publicity is to be avoided if at all possible. If a one-on-one confrontation is successful, no further steps will be necessary; more importantly "you have gained your brother" (v. 15). As a second step, the guilty member is to be protected by entrusting the investigation to a small group of two or three members who will accurately weigh the evidence and provide dependable testimony. This would exclude the possibility of assassination by gossip— something that can easily happen in a close-knit religious group. The witness of only one accuser is inadequate; the accused has a right to an impartial hearing by at least two members. If these first two steps fail, a meeting of the congregation should be called in the hope that the offenders will accept its authority (for similar situations, 1 Cor. 5—6). Such a meeting constitutes a last resort, the purpose of which is to accomplish a reconciliation. Failing that, exclusion by the church would correspond to the member's own rejection of the church's authority.

Even in this extreme case, however, the congregation's action must conform to quite definite specifications. There must be full agreement. The church must be gathered "in my name," a requirement that is not easy to meet, and it must fully consult the gracious Lord who is "in the midst." Finally, it must recognize that all earthly actions derive their importance only from what happens in heaven, from what God does there (v. 19).

Scholars are largely in agreement that these first efforts at "canon law" developed in the church only after the death of Jesus. Does this make them inauthentic? Does it destroy their authority? Not if the risen Lord continues to be found in the midst of a community gathered in his name. Not if its efforts at self-discipline are expressions of the humility that is indigenous to prayer to the Father of Jesus. Not if the logic of the following parable informs the church's action at every step.

HOMILETICAL INTERPRETATION

There are a number of options which persons have when they have been wronged by another, or when they see another involved in evil which harms themselves and others. Vengeance appears to be a highly attractive option. It seems almost an instinctive reaction to want to strike back at someone who has hurt us. The desire to get even seems to be deeply ingrained within most of us. Furthermore, we can find good justification for seeking vengeance; the other person really needs to be taught a lesson so that the evil acts will not continue. It is only fair that there should be a retribution when we have been hurt, and with such an argument we can appeal to high principles of justice. Paul's words in today's lessons, echoing a clear statement of Jesus', speaks against that option: "Repay no one evil for evil. . . . Beloved, never avenge yourselves."

Another option in handling those who have wronged us is total separation. We make no overt effort to strike back, but we simply isolate ourselves. We want nothing to do with those who have offended us or stolen from us or cheated us.

A third option is to do nothing. We take no action against the other. We try to go on as though nothing had happened. We simply refuse to deal with the fact that an offense has been committed and a wrong done.

Not only does the biblical witness speak powerfully against the way of vengeance, it also has some more positive options to press than either isolating ourselves or ignoring what has happened. Three other possibilities are suggested by the texts for today: confront those who do evil, repay evil with good, and discern the difficult relationship in the context of God's care and purpose.

First Lesson: Ezek. 33:7–11. Ezekiel described the prophet's role in terms of the watchman who is charged to give warning to the people, and noted the heavy responsibility put upon the prophet. He was to warn the wicked to turn from their ways, and if he failed he would be held accountable even to the loss of his own life. There is something abrasive and even offensive about the person who takes the task of warning others about their wickedness, and prophets were not noted for their popularity with the people to whom God had sent them. But God had called prophets to warn the people that they might turn from their wickedness and escape the death which was coming upon them.

Although we are not OT prophets, the word of the Lord to the prophet is a word to us as we care for our nation, our community, our church, our family. It is hard and risky to speak the warning to others about the wrongs they are doing, yet we are called to make judgments and to speak out when we see others destroying themselves and their families with blind ambition, when we see hatred poisoning their lives, when we see them committing affronts which corrupt their relationships.

Gospel: Matt. 18:15–20. The Gospel also speaks of the importance of confronting others who have sinned against us. "If your brother sins against you, go and tell him his fault, between you and him alone." If that encounter does not heal the breach, then take witnesses, for the dynamics of relationships between two people are changed in the presence of others. If that does not succeed, then involve the church. To confront others is to take them seriously, and opens the possibility of their turning from the wrong they are doing. But surely the confrontation is needed for our own welfare as well, to enable us to deal with the hurt and the pain and the anger.

Second Lesson: Rom. 12:9–21. Paul warned against vengeance, against repaying evil with evil. In those assertions he does echo the words of Jesus who admonished, "Do not resist one who is evil" (Matt. 5:39). Some people hear a kind of passivity in those words, as though evil were simply to be allowed to continue unchecked. Paul is much more dynamic and positive than that. He wants us to move aggressively against the evil with the good.

Paul sets forth a number of ways in which the good is to be expressed in meeting and overcoming the evil. We are to "let love be genuine." Love for those who have wronged us involves deep concern for their welfare, and anguish for what they are doing to themselves in the evil they are doing to us. We are to "be patient in tribulation," to develop the capacity to seek the right moment and the right way in which the healing between us and our adversary might take place. We are to "bless those who persecute" us, to seek the ways in which, through us, their blighted lives might be restored to health. We are to "take thought for what is noble in the sight of all," to seek those ways in which the dignity and the image of God in our opponent can be affirmed and enhanced. Evil is to be opposed and fought with all the vigor of which we are capable, but it is to be repaid with good and not with more evil.

Dealing with the evil in others and confronting those who sin against us makes awesome demands on us. How can we bear that kind of burden in our human relationships? Surely it can be done only in the context of discerning our human relationships as under God. The prophet did not set out on his own to warn his people about their wicked ways, but saw his task as a calling laid upon him by God.

Paul also relates what he has to say about our efforts to meet evil with good to the crucial concern of our relationship with God. He was not just offering good advice about how to get along well with our neighbors, but was calling his readers to "be aglow with the Spirit," and to "serve the

Lord." Out of constancy in prayer we may find the sensitivity and the strength to make creative response to the sin which we confront.

In the gospel account of the way in which the church deals with the effect of sin between persons, people are not left to deal with one another simply on a human level of struggling to settle their differences. The church gets involved, the church which seeks to manifest on earth that which is done by the Father in heaven, the church which gathers in the name of Christ, the church which finds its life in the conviction that Christ indeed is still in its midst.

The Seventeenth Sunday after Pentecost

Lutheran	Roman Catholic	Episcopal	Pres/UCC/Chr	Meth/COCU
Gen. 50:15–21	Sir. 27:30—28:7	Sir. 27:30—28:7	Gen. 4:13–16	Gen. 50:15–21 or Sir. 27:30—28:7
Rom. 14:5–9	Rom. 14:7–9	Rom. 14:5–12	Rom. 14:5–9	Rom. 14:5–12
Matt. 18:21–35	Matt. 18:21–35	Matt. 18:21–35	Matt. 18:21–35	Matt. 18:21–35

EXEGESIS

First Lesson: Sir. 27:30—28:7. Before studying any passage in this book, the interpreter should read the prologue, in which the author indicates the purpose of his work. Sirach is a collection of the teachings of many Hebrew sages, conveying the basic moral standards of Israel. No passage is more typical than this, and none was more widely adopted by early Christian teachers. The wise men were surgeons of the human heart, and this passage could be labeled the anatomy of anger.

Person *A* is angered by Person *B*, whom he believes has injured him. This anger produces a distortion in *A's* vision. *A* attributes to *B* a guilt that fully merits punishment. *A* assumes his own innocence, and therefore his right to compensation for the unjustified injury (whether or not he uses the term revenge, he is more likely to use the term justice). *A's* anger against *B* is immediately transferred to advisors who do not share *A's* anger and his claim to justice. This anger is especially turned against any third party, human or divine, which commands him to forgive *B*. Anger interprets such forgiveness as a confession either of weakness on

A's part or of vindication of *B's* sin. So anger proliferates until it fills the entire horizon of *A's* world; it infects that world with illness. It induces *A* to suppose that God himself is angry with *B*, and that *B's* sin guarantees God's vengeance on *B* rather than on *A*. Consequently *A's* conception of God is determined by his anger with *B*.

The wise man is not only perceptive in his anatomy of anger but also in his remedies for it. His basic truth is that "all wisdom comes from the Lord" (Sir. 1:1). A corollary is the flat statement that anger is sin. The desire for vengeance is an abomination, deluding the person obsessed by it. *A* cannot expect healing from the Lord as long as he identifies such healing with vengeance on *B*. His very desire for vengeance excludes such healing. Healing is equivalent to forgiveness; only in being merciful does any person receive mercy. When *A* forgives *B* he will make peace not only with *B*, but with himself and with his God, with God's covenant and commandments, and with the true end of his own life. The person who remembers that end will receive the grace to replace enmity with mercy.

All this understanding of the human heart is packed into this small cluster of words. Small wonder that Jesus and Paul absorbed it so fully.

Second Lesson: Rom. 14:5–12. This passage shows how fully Paul's thinking was controlled by his theology and his Christology. God is the Father "from whom are all things and for whom we exist." Jesus Christ is the one "through whom are all things and through whom we exist" (1 Cor. 8:6). In the passage at hand we may see how Paul applied those convictions to acute disputes within the Roman churches over diet and over holy days. To him the honoring of the Lord was far more important than observing the Sabbath (cf. Isa. 56). When a believer treats all days alike in honor of the Lord, that fact makes every day holy. When one person gives thanks while eating only kosher food, and another person gives thanks while eating all foods (cf. Mark 7:1–23), the bond of unity created by their gratitude to the Lord becomes stronger than any tension created by their divergent practices. If one person dies, but another lives on, does even that division count? Not at all, since both belong to the same Lord, who claims the allegiance of both. Such temporal matters as birth and death do not affect the strength of that bond. And if that is true of a person's dying, it surely must be true of such matters as food and religious observances of all kinds.

Vv. 7–9 in our text were absolutely decisive in Paul's thinking, yet they were quite ignored both in the Roman churches and in later centuries. They are supremely relevant to every funeral service, though they are seldom used. They contain a profound conception of what God actually accomplished in Jesus' death and resurrection. They describe concisely the meaning of faith. They set the compass for charting each day's journey—and all this within three verses that are so constructed as to be easily memorized and kept near the surface of one's mind for instant reference. Each person has an autobiography, and that autobiography has a beginning and an end. He measures the importance of daily experiences by their bearing on that beginning and end. These verses redefine those ultimate horizons. It was because Paul set every story within these wider brackets—living and dying to the Lord—that his moral teachings became so distinctive and so impelling.

Gospel: Matt. 18:21–35. This evangelist was especially interested in Peter, yet he was no hero-worshiper. In chap. 16, as we have seen, he pictures this apostle as the spokesman for both God and Satan. Now, in telling a story which in Luke (17:4) makes no mention of this apostle, Matthew makes Peter the dialogue partner of Jesus. This is entirely appropriate in this case because the subject is forgiveness and because Jesus had earlier bestowed on Peter the power of the keys. The warning of v. 35 is especially applicable to the use of that power. It is also applicable to the deliberations of a church court in dealing with an obstreperous member: Even when excommunication is found necessary, forgiveness "from your heart" remains obligatory. In the parable we have Matthew's answer to the question: How is Jesus present among those gathered in his name? Answer: If he is present in the authority to condemn, he is also present in the practice of unlimited forgiveness (whether the text reads 77 or 490 times, the meaning is the same).

Like most other parables, this story has received much sentimental praise for its beauty and power. Many who praise it never stop to examine the difficulties caused by its steel-trap logic. Consider two such difficulties. The first difficulty ensues whenever any church tries to enforce the disciplinary procedures of Matt. 18:15–20 and at the same time tries to obey the parable's insistence on unlimited forgiveness. How can any human jury order the punishment of a serious crime and yet avoid God's punishment of the servant who is delivered to the jailers until he pays his debt? A second difficulty is this: Both in the case of discipline and in the parable itself, it is clear that one person has suffered unjustly from another person's actions. In neither case, however, is any concern shown for preserving the rights of that person. Did not Jesus nor Matthew have regard for the claims of justice? Is the servant of v. 28

never entitled to the payment of debts owed to him? If not, can any religious institution, let alone any secular society, survive if the non-payment of obligations becomes standard procedure?

Such difficulties are built into the parable, perhaps with malice aforethought. They call attention to a presupposition, without which the parable becomes nonsensical. That presupposition is the king's initial forgiveness of the first servant's debt, a debt (let us suppose) of ten million dollars. That is the point of the parable that is hardest to believe. But if that point is accepted as something that has actually happened, the logic of the teaching becomes inescapable.

HOMILETICAL INTERPRETATION

Paul asks the questions: "Why do you pass judgment on your brother?" or "You—why do you despise your brother?" There are many possible responses to those questions and many legitimate answers related to the specific circumstances in which people find themselves. In his letter to the Romans, Paul was dealing with the situation in which people were antagonistic toward each other over matters of principle. They were arguing over the appropriate food to eat. They were disagreeing about holy days and how to observe them. These were matters of serious import, having to do with what the people believed to be fundamental religious convictions. They passed judgment on one another because they believed that significant issues were at stake. It is then possible to argue that people who do wrong must be punished because evil must be restrained and they must learn that they cannot wrong others with impunity. Judgments must be made and punishment must be meted out in order to restrain those who would harm others to their own benefit. Or again it can be argued that vengeance is the "natural" response of persons when they have been hurt by others. It seems to be instinctive for persons to strike back at those who have wronged them, to seek ways to get even with those who have taken from them. If persons are going to maintain their integrity and keep their sense of self-worth, they must be willing to fight back against those who would violate their person or take their property. In the long story of human relationships, the quest for vengeance is a basic and repeated occurrence.

Finally, persons stand in judgment on others and despise others simply because those others are different. For many people, anything different from the norms and mores to which they are accustomed poses a threat. They have difficulty in accepting the validity of different styles and standards. In order to establish the legitimacy of their own ways and the superiority of their own standards, they condemn the ways and the standards of those who differ from them.

First Lesson: Sir. 27:30—28:7. Persons who take it upon themselves to judge others and who seek vengeance run grave risks. The biblical accounts make clear the heavy price to be paid by those who take the way of vengeance. Persons pay the price of vengeance and judgment in terms of what happens to their own lives. Jesus, the son of Sirach, author of Ecclesiasticus, puts it in this way: "Anger and wrath, these also are abominations, and the sinful man will possess them." Life is corrupted and diminished when persons allow themselves to be consumed by hatred and anger toward others. A recent newspaper report gave the account of a man whose father had been killed by a hit-and-run driver. The son had been driven by a desire for vengeance, so that for ten years he had spent every possible moment and used every available resource to find the driver of the car. At last he had the satisfaction of venting his hatred on the man who had killed his father. How many rich things he had missed in life because for ten years he had devoted his time and energy solely to seeking vengeance! No matter what the provocation, anger and wrath are abominations.

Gospel: Matt. 18:21–35. To stand in judgment on others distorts the relationship with them. To seek vengeance cuts off all possibility of creative relationship between the avenger and the one against whom vengeance is sought. When the forgiven servant in the story of Jesus refused to forgive his fellow servant and had him put in prison, nothing good could happen between those two men.

Those who take upon themselves the role of judge of the lives and actions of others open themselves to the risks of arrogance and make meaningful interaction difficult indeed. When a person has wronged another, there is no way that the relationship between them can be restored unless there is forgiveness.

Vengeance also creates disaster in our relationship to God. "He that takes vengeance will suffer vengeance from the Lord. . . . Forgive your neighbor the wrong he has done, and then your sins will be pardoned when you pray. Does a man harbor anger against another, and yet seek for healing from the Lord?" The conviction of Jesus, son of Sirach, that the way in which persons deal with those who have wronged them is crucial for the way in which God deals with them is confirmed by Jesus of Nazareth when he declared at the end of his story about the unforgiving servant: "So also my heavenly Father will do to every one of you, if you do not forgive your brother from your heart."

Persons who pronounce judgment on others will find themselves under the judgment of God. Persons who let hatred for others fester in their lives cannot know the healing grace of God within their own lives. Persons who will not forgive cannot accept the forgiveness of God for the sin in their lives.

Second Lesson: Rom. 14:5–12. Paul deals specifically with the issue of making judgments when people believe that crucial issues are at stake. Principles are important, but Paul reminds his readers that they are not to serve principles but to serve God. "He who observes the day, observes it in honor of the Lord." People are to remember that they belong to the Lord, and that Christ lived and died that they might belong to the Lord in life and in death. They are to remember that those who differ with them on matters of principle and practice also belong to the Lord, and to acknowledge that in their practice they are trying to honor the Lord. People within the faith will certainly differ with each other, but judgments take on a different meaning when they are made with the recognition that all have a common loyalty to God, and that all shall "stand before the judgment seat of God."

All three of these lessons deal with the way in which judgment and forgiveness can be offered, and the crucial precedence of persons over principles. It does not matter how often a person sins, forgiveness is to be offered.

How is it possible for persons to forgive with such grace and generosity? Both Jesus, son of Sirach, and Jesus Christ relate the call for forgiveness to the fundamental *human* situation before God. "Remember the end of your life, and cease from enmity, remember destruction and death, and be true to the commandments." Jesus tells the story of the king who forgave an enormous amount to the servant who refused to forgive a small amount to his fellow servant. The point is that persons misread their situation if they see themselves as the innocent who are being asked to forgive the guilty. Those called upon to forgive are those who have been forgiven by God. The grace to forgive others becomes possible when people know the grace of forgiveness which has been offered to them by God. Only with perception of God's relationship to us does it become possible to judge with mercy and to forgive with grace.

The Eighteenth Sunday after Pentecost

Lutheran	Roman Catholic	Episcopal	Pres/UCC/Chr	Meth/COCU
Isa. 55:6–9	Isa. 55:6–9	Jon. 3:10—4:11	Isa. 55:6–11	Isa. 55:6–11
Phil. 1:1–5 (6–11), 19–27	Phil. 1:20c–24, 27a	Phil. 1:21–27	Phil. 1:21–27	Phil. 1:1–11, 19–27
Matt. 20:1–16	Matt. 20:1–16	Matt. 20:1–16	Matt. 20:1–16	Matt. 20:1–16

EXEGESIS

First Lesson: Isa. 55:6–9. This passage is worth studying as an example of the basic principles of Hebrew poetry. In vv. 6–7, one notes three couplets in which the second line repeats in different words the same thought as the first line. This is known as *synonymous parallelism.* Seeking the Lord (line a) is an action similar to calling upon him (line b); the nearness of the Lord (line b) means that he can now be found (line a). What makes this passage a superb call to worship is the fact that God is himself addressing everyone who is thirsty (v. 1). This call to worship in v. 6 is paralleled in v. 7 by its ethical equivalent: To seek the Lord (v. 6, line a) requires that the wicked worshiper forsake his present way (v. 7, line b). One cannot truly seek this Lord without confessing one's sin and relying upon his pardon.

In vv. 8–9, a new element enters, that of antithesis and contrast. In v. 8 line *a* contrasts the thoughts of God and the thoughts of the worshiper while line *b* contrasts their ways. This is called *antithetical parallelism;* the poetic balance is used to stress an antithesis, although the contrast in line *a* is again synonymous with the contrast in line *b*. Similarities are employed to underscore the wide contrast between man's wickedness and God's mercy. By implication this suggests that a man's thoughts are made unrighteous by his refusal to be as merciful as God.

Still another type of Hebrew rhythm is called the *chiasmus.* In this case the order of parallel ideas is reversed: a, b, b, a. In v. 7 the sequence is from *ways* to *thoughts;* in v. 8 that order is reversed and moves from *thoughts* to *ways.* In v. 9 the sequence is again reversed. The literary construction serves to lead the reader's attention to the wide disparity between the attitudes of heaven and earth. It prepares him for the descriptions in vv. 10ff. of how God's thoughts and ways operate to execute his forgiveness on earth. Much more is involved than a liturgical call to worship; there is a call to revise one's former conceptions of God's relationship to the whole world.

Second Lesson: Phil. 1:1–5, 19–27. This letter makes clear the situation of both the author and his audience. Paul is author; there is no doubt of that. Nor is there any doubt of the audience: the earliest gentile congregation in what is now Europe. Paul was writing from prison (1:13) to a group of his converts who have also been called "to suffer for the sake of Christ" (1:29). Both apostle and congregation are engaged in the same conflict and tempted to be frightened by their opponents (1:28). The fact of suffering has produced opposite effects among different people. On the one hand, some Christians have been made bolder by Paul's example to preach the gospel (1:14) and for this he is grateful. His imprisonment has also called the attention of his captors to the gospel of Christ. Then, too, the readiness of some churchmen in Philippi to accept violence has encouraged others to do so. On the other hand, this widespread suffering has alarmed and frightened many, and one should be sympathetic with them. Some leaders in Philippi were taking advantage of Paul's imprisonment to suggest that something was wrong with both his message and his character (a likely inference from 1:15–17). These same leaders were no doubt trying to avoid further conflicts with the non-Christian public. Thus the courage of one group was increasing the fears of the other group, and this destroyed the morale of the entire community.

Paul realized that the crucial question was how seriously all of them should take the threat of death. Paul's answer is given in v. 21: They should all accept the possibility that their dying would be a gain. Why so? Because a martyred disciple would show honor to a martyred Messiah (v. 20). Because in such a death the disciple would "depart and be with Christ" (v. 23). Because his courage under attack would be an authentic way of proclaiming the gospel. However, if in spite of such hostility Paul or his followers were spared, their continued living could also be a form of honoring Christ. They could carry on fruitful work, not for their own sakes but for the sake of others (vv. 24f.). All this would be true if they fully accepted the threat of death. Otherwise, to buy more years of life because they were afraid of death would be forever to their shame (v. 20). In all this Paul took Jesus as his model, and he urged the Philippians to do the same. They should unite in the desire to be worthy of Christ's gospel (v. 27). If they did that they would discover that the opposite of living in fear is a life of joy (v. 19).

Gospel: Matt. 20:1–16. This text illustrates many features of the parable as a mode of teaching. The parable was used in oral rather than written discourse, passing from mouth to ear rather than from page to eye. It often attracted attention by depicting an action that was abnormal or eccentric. Some parables did not require a punch line to indicate the point (for example, Matt. 13:44). Others required such a "moral" that would make quite explicit why the story was told. This was true of the parable at hand, for the teller had to make clear the reason for the strange action of this employer. Since this parable had had many tellers before it was "embalmed" in writing, four of these tellers have left their signatures on the parable in the form of their explanations. The story itself ends with v. 12. Beginning with v. 13 we find four somewhat different answers to the protest of the workers. Which of the four fits the story most closely?

The first reply of the employer is in v. 13. He has done his workers no wrong, but has paid them what he promised. There may seem to have been inequality in wages, but no injustice. Is this an adequate point for the story? It seems to be weaker than the story itself. So a second explanation may be found in v. 14b and v. 15. The action of the employer is defended in terms of his right to use his money in any way he sees fit. Landowners have their money; they should take it and spend it as they will. This man has chosen a strange way to spend his, but that is his right. This explanation fits the story yet it throws little light on the motives of the employer, who surely is meant to represent God. We turn then to the third explanation, which takes the form of the brief question in v. 15b, with its sharp barb. The employer's generosity is opposed to the employees' stinginess. By implication God's grace is the opposite of human selfishness. This explanation is not only an adequate point for the human story; it points in the direction of the basic truth of the gospel. The fourth explanation (v. 16) by comparison seems quite out of place and has probably been borrowed from other passages (Matt. 19:30; Luke 13:30).

We should thus recall four different ways in which different preachers and teachers used the basic story in the decades before Matthew. It is probably true that no preacher can use the story without adding his own interpretation. The context—the time, the place, the purposes, the desired results of his sermon—will impart a fresh nuance to the story itself. What answer would you have had the employer give to his disgruntled workers? He could have quoted from Isa. 55:9, "My ways are higher than your ways," or from Rom. 11:34, "Who had known the mind of the Lord?" In the end, the test of parable interpretation is how well a particular explanation calls attention to the mysterious generosity of the kingdom of heaven (Matt. 20:1).

HOMILETICAL INTERPRETATION

At the beginning of his epic poem, *Paradise Lost,* John Milton appealed to the Spirit for aid in the task to which he had set himself:

> What in me is dark
> Illumine, what is low raise and support;
> That to the height of this great argument
> I may assert eternal Providence,
> And justify the ways of God to men.

All three texts which we are considering here raise issues about what God is doing, and provoke questions about the ways of God. We need not be so bold as to make Milton's claim. But these texts do address some of the questions which are raised as we seek to discern what God is doing.

First Lesson: Isa. 55:6–9. This word of God through the prophet refutes any effort to explain God and his ways in human terms, and those are the only terms which we have available to us. "For my thoughts are not your thoughts, neither are your ways my ways, says the Lord." This word of the Lord sets the limits on what we can understand and explain about the ways of God. We dare not reduce the divine will and purpose to the human scale. We may try to understand the ways of God using such human notions as justice, equality, fairness, success, happiness, and fulfillment; but no human terms are fully transferable to the divine. In all our talk about God, this warning must be central: "For my thoughts are not your thoughts, neither are your ways my ways, says the Lord."

It might appear, then, that the best admonition would be to forget the whole enterprise of seeking to know and understand the ways of God. But that is not what the prophet declares. Rather his word is "Seek the Lord while he may be found, call upon him while he is near." God is beyond all human thought, and yet we are able to discern something of who he is and what he does. God is the Wholly Other, the Unknown, the Mystery, and yet he is available to us and we can know him.

An analogy from human relationships may help us to grasp something of what it means to talk about knowing God. We know other persons at many levels. Some we know simply by sight, and have only a superficial acquaintance with them. Other people we know more intimately, and have a sense of who they are and how they approach life and what they value. A husband and wife know each other in ways that two people do not if their relationship is limited to saying "Good morning." But even a

husband and wife do not know all about each other. They cannot explain
who the other is and why the other behaves in certain ways. There is a
hidden depth of mystery in every human being, even in those we know
best. In some such fashion it is meaningful to talk about knowing God,
even while we declare that his ways are not our ways and his thoughts
are not our thoughts.

Two things may be noted about the word of the prophet. First, some
initiative and responsibility rests with those who would know God. God
is not an object to be found, and we can know him only because he has
chosen to make himself known to us. But we must seek to know him, we
must call upon him. We are invited to pay attention to the activity of God
in the world around us, to be sensitive to the gentle presence of God in
our lives, to listen to the word which God speaks to us. For us as
Christians, above all we are called to ponder the coming of God in the life
and death, the words and ministry of Jesus Christ.

Second, knowing God has to do with the direction and intent of our
lives. "Let the wicked forsake his way, and the unrighteous man his
thoughts." Knowing God is neither a solely intellectual exercise nor
purely emotional encounter. Knowing God involves repentance, a turning from evil ways and corrupt thoughts. God is beyond the thoughts of
persons, but as we are able to distinguish good from evil, right from
wrong, love from hate, truth from falsehood, we can affirm that good and
right and love and truth are of God.

Second Lesson: Phil. 1:1–5, 19–27. The exegesis of this passage
probes in an effort to discern some of the concerns in the church of
Philippi which led Paul to write as he did. It points out that some of the
leaders in the church there seemed to have viewed Paul's imprisonment
as evidence that something must be wrong with him or with what he was
doing. The expectation that faithful service to God will result in tangible
reward is a common view as persons reflect on the ways of God. In such
a view of the way in which God deals with persons, failure or tragedy
must be the punishment which is deserved for wrongs done.

Inspired by the witness of Jesus Christ, Paul offers a quite different
interpretation of what is happening to him, and of the kind of life which
issues from faithfulness to God. The external circumstances are not
crucial in deciding whether a person has been faithful. Jesus went to his
death not because he had failed to be responsible to the will of God, but
precisely because he had been obedient. Paul was in prison not because
God was punishing him for his failures, but because he had been faithful
in his witness.

He writes to the Philippians: "I want you to know, brethren, that what has happened to me has really served to advance the gospel" (Phil. 1:12). Paul declares that whether he lives or whether he dies, "now as always Christ will be honored in my body." If he lives he can continue to minister to them in "fruitful labor." If he dies he will be with Christ.

God's blessings are richer and broader than our human views of success and happiness. It is his blessing that whatever happens to us, life or death, success or failure, can be the occasion for faithful response to his love and growing relationship with him. Paul points to the possibilities whatever the circumstance when he writes to the Philippians: "Only let your manner of life be worthy of the gospel of Christ."

There is mystery in the way in which God deals with us, but through Jesus Christ we along with Paul can know that even death is not the ultimate threat but the final promise. "For to me to live is Christ, and to die is gain."

Gospel: Matt. 20:1–16. The principle of fairness is one of the standards which people use in their dealings with each other. And if we want to hold ourselves and others to some standard of fairness, it seems appropriate to apply this principle to our expectation of the way in which God deals with his people. Surely we should expect God to be fair in the ways in which he treats people.

But the parable of Jesus makes clear that the principle of fairness does not exactly apply to the ways of God. There is something inherently unfair in the notion of grace. It does not seem fair that the people who worked only one hour in the vineyard got as much for their labor as the people who worked all day in the hot sun, although the story makes clear that the owner paid the first workers the full amount he had agreed to; God does not demand that persons earn the blessing which he bestows. The grace and the love of God transcend our human assessments of what is fair, and we cannot bind God nor understand God solely in terms of the principle of fairness.

We can identify readily with the first workers, for we too are quick to note when others seem to be getting blessings which do not come to us. But the parable poses the crucial question in our relationship with the God of grace: "Or do you begrudge my generosity?" Can we see blessings which come to others and give thanks for them? Can we move beyond questions of what persons deserve to praise God for the good which has been given? If we live with the God of grace, then we rejoice when undeserved blessings come to us and to others.

The Nineteenth Sunday after Pentecost

Lutheran	Roman Catholic	Episcopal	Pres/UCC/Chr	Meth/COCU
Ezek. 18:1–4, 25–32	Ezek. 18:25–28	Ezek. 18:1–4, 25–32	Ezek. 18:25–29	Ezek. 18:1–4, 25–32
Phil. 2:1–5 (6–11)	Phil. 2:1–11 or Phil. 2:1–5	Phil. 2:1–13	Phil. 2:1–11	Phil. 2:1–13
Matt. 21:28–32	Matt. 21:28–32	Matt. 21:28–32	Matt. 21:28–32	Matt. 21:28–32

EXEGESIS

First Lesson: Ezek. 18:1–4, 25–32. Ezekiel was assigned four tasks by the God who appointed him a prophet. First of all, he had to destroy the clever evasions by which people try to escape responsibility for their own actions. A typical evasion, then as now, was to explain the sins of one generation by referring to the sins of the parents (vv. 1–4). A person can always trace the origins of his misdeeds to influences from outside himself. To use that alibi, however, is to defy the truth that every person belongs to God and must answer directly to him and to no one else (v. 4). The corollary of this truth is the recognition that to sin against God is to die.

A second task of the prophet is to call his people to take the next "right turning." Have they sinned? He must tell them that no iniquity is so great as to make impossible such a turning. Have they been righteous? He must warn them that in their self-confidence they are in danger of turning away from God. Every moment is the moment for turning; life and death are determined by the direction toward which one turns (vv. 26–27).

The prophet is summoned, in the third place, to defend the justice of God's rule against the constant complaints of his people. They expect God to turn toward them, forgetting their failures to turn toward God. For whatever happens they lay the blame on God (vv. 25–29), judging his behavior by whether their affairs prosper. He must be measured by their standards of right and wrong, justice and injustice. His ways must be like theirs. But that is an illusion which the prophet must destroy.

In destroying that illusion, however, the prophet must disclose more clearly what God's ways actually are, that is, what he demands of them. Ezekiel tries to do this in vv. 5–13. Here he makes it clear that to turn back to God is to turn away from all forms of pride and self-concern and to turn toward others, placing their rights and needs ahead of one's own. Here Ezekiel defines life (v. 9) primarily in terms of obeying his equivalent of the Golden Rule. This is God's form of justice which men find it so hard to comprehend. And that is why the task of the prophet never ends.

Second Lesson: Phil. 2:1–13. Discussions of Pauline Christology sooner or later come to deal with vv. 6–11, and there is no end to scholarly debates on the origin and meaning of this "hymn." Was this in fact a hymn before Paul incorporated it? If so, where did it originate? In a pre-Pauline Hellenistic church? in a non-Christian gnostic community? (for which, of course the reference to the cross would need to be removed). V. 7 speaks of the self-emptying of Christ. What precisely is the meaning of this *kenosis*? What does the hymn imply with regard to the preexistence and the postexistence of Christ? Theological problems proliferate in all directions, and there is little consensus on the answers.

The exegete should recognize that Paul's primary concern was not with the details of the hymn but with problems emerging in the Philippian church. In his judgment the solution of those problems required a "mind" and a quality of life more consistent with their faith in Christ Jesus (vv. 1–5). The function of the hymn is to help them work out their own salvation in the light of God's "good pleasure" (vv. 12–13). Only by making contact with this intention of Paul can we do justice to his thought. Ethical dilemmas are the key here to his theology.

Furthermore, for both Paul and his readers, these ethical issues were inseparable from political issues. First of all there is the thorny thicket of church politics, present in every congregation. Throughout this epistle Paul was dealing with sharp divisions among Philippian Christians (1:15–17). They were not united by one spirit (1:27) in their defense and confirmation of the gospel (1:7). The heat generated by these altercations comes to the surface in the explosion of 3:2ff. In fact it is safe to assume that each exhortation in 2:1–5 was prompted by church practice; for example, members were inclined to do everything from conceit (v. 3). Moreover, as we have seen, the problems of internal politics had been aggravated by the relationship of the church to the surrounding society. Fear of sufferings (like those of Christ [Phil. 2:8] and those of Paul [Phil. 3:8]) had induced some leaders to seek an easier accommodation to the mood of the city. Then, as always, it was political pressures that engendered "fear and trembling"; that is why Paul was so insistent on writing that God was at work in them. The function of the Christ-hymn in vv. 6–11 was to make clear how God could accomplish his good pleasure and their salvation under those very conditions.

Gospel: Matt. 21:28–32. Many of Jesus' parables were probably told in the midst of controversy, as a debater's weapon against his opponents. That may well have been true of last week's parable. The generosity of the employer was a rebuke to the stinginess of the first set of employees (Matt. 20:1–16). It certainly is true of today's parable. It appears in the midst of the deadly warfare between the chief priests and elders on the one side, and John the Baptist and Jesus on the other. At stake in this strife is the allegiance of the multitude (vv. 23–27). An outcome of this war was the death of the two prophets (vv. 34–39) and also the death of "those miserable wretches" (v. 41). As Matthew saw it, the parable of the two sons was a weapon in this warfare; through using it Jesus succeeded in getting his enemies to condemn themselves (v. 31).

It is possible, however, to separate the parable from its use as a weapon. The parable itself ends with the question of v. 31a. If we confine our attention to that core (vv. 28–31a), we will note that it conveys several important insights into human behavior. For example, both sons were self-deceived. Because neither son really knew himself, his prediction concerning future action was mistaken. Neither father nor son should rely too heavily upon such predictions. Moreover, the parable repeats the insight of Ezekiel 18: It is always possible for a son to change his mind; he can always turn from disobedience to obedience, or from filial loyalty to disloyalty. Thus the parable warns against trusting too much in good intentions, with which the road to hell is smoothly paved. Insights of this sort make the parable useful in many situations. Probably every preacher has used it often, sometimes with good results.

In Matthew's case, however, the situation transformed the simple parable into an allegory. The father stands for God, whose call to work is relayed first by John and then by Jesus. The son who first refused to work, but afterward repented, represents the tax collectors and harlots, who repented as they responded to the preaching of the two prophets, and who entered the vineyard (the kingdom of heaven). The second son represents the leaders of Israel, the chief priests and elders, whose promise to work in God's vineyard has been broken by their refusal to heed the call of John and Jesus. That promise had been broken three times, according to Matthew's reading of previous history: they had refused to respond to John's call; even when they had seen the multitude of sinners repenting at the message of John, they had stubbornly refused to repent (v. 32); finally, they had killed God's own son (v. 39). In Matthew's version of the parable of the two sons, it becomes more than a parable with general religious and moral implications; it even becomes more than an allegory with a contemporary equivalent for each actor, an equivalent reflecting Matthew's own warfare with the synagogue rulers of his own day. It becomes a penetrating epitome of the story of John, the story of Jesus, the story of Israel, and we should also probably say, the story of the Christian church.

HOMILETICAL INTERPRETATION

The texts for this week stress a different perspective on the truth about people and their relationship with God from that which was stressed in the texts for last week. Ezekiel talks about the death which shall come to the person who commits iniquity, and stresses the justice of the ways in which God deals with righteous and with evil individuals. Paul talks about persons working out their "own salvation with fear and trembling." The story which Jesus tells about the two sons points to the necessity of doing the work which God asks. What individual persons are and what they do is genuinely significant in their relationship with God. The biblical witness confronts us with the paradox of God's generous and gracious love, and of his rigorous demand for righteousness and obedience. In seeking to interpret the nature and meaning of our relationship with God, both the grace and the demand must be clearly affirmed.

First Lesson: Ezek. 18:1–4, 25–32. The words of Ezekiel lift up one side of another paradox. Speaking what he claims to be the word of the Lord to him, Ezekiel declares: "What do you mean by repeating this proverb concerning the land of Israel, 'The fathers have eaten sour grapes, and the children's teeth are set on edge'? As I live, says the Lord God, this proverb shall no more be used by you in Israel."

Surely there is evidence that the old proverb, so like the Lord's declaration that he would "visit the iniquity of the father upon the children" spoken as part of the Ten Commandments, has validity as we seek to understand what happens to persons in our own time. When one generation exploits and plunders the land, the consequences will be suffered by generations as yet unborn. When one generation sows the seeds of bitterness and hatred in dealing with an oppressed people, their sons and daughters will fight the wars which ensue. The iniquity of the fathers and mothers is indeed visited upon the children, even to the third and fourth generation, and persons indeed are profoundly influenced by the impact of their environment.

Yet Ezekiel declares that this proverb shall no longer be used in Israel, and that "the wickedness of the wicked shall be upon himself" (Ezek.

18:20). Persons *are* shaped by their heritage. But they are also responsible for what they do. We must not deny their essential humanity. They are responsible beings and must bear the burden of responsibility for what they do. They are held accountable before God. "Behold, all souls are mine; the soul of the father as well as the soul of the son is mine." In seeking to interpret the human situation, both the impact of the sins of the fathers and the essential responsibility of persons for their own lives before God must be clearly affirmed.

Gospel: Matthew 21:28–32. Jesus' story about the sons speaks clear warning about the risk, inadequacy, and frailty of good intentions. We have not been righteous before God simply because we think that the good ought to be done. The parable threatens all of us, for how often have we substituted good intention for good actions in defining our faithfulness to God. Yet neither we nor those who heard the parable as Jesus spoke it have any difficulty in answering the question which Jesus put: "Which of the two did the will of his father?" We agree with the chief priests and the elders who readily responded that the obedient son was the one who did what his father told him, not the one who said he would and then did not.

There may be no surprises in the story which Jesus told about the two sons, but Matthew's account of this whole encounter between Jesus and the Jewish officials moves on to a real shocker. Who are those who do what the father asks? The chief priests and elders would have been quite clear about that. They considered themselves the obedient ones. They went beyond lip service. They did what God wanted his people to do: they obeyed the law, lived righteous lives, kept isolated from the unclean. But listen to Jesus: "Truly, I say to you, the tax collectors and the harlots go into the kingdom of God before you." That judgment puts a wholly different interpretation on the story of the two sons. The obedient son is not the one who keeps all the laws, who upholds all the principles, who avoids contamination with the impure and the outcasts. The tax collectors and the harlots would hardly qualify on those terms. The tax collectors and the harlots were like the first son. It was the sense of their own need and the openness to the love offered them which got them into the kingdom of heaven.

There is a continuing paradox between the freely offered grace of God and the demands that persons be faithful and obedient. But in seeking to heed the demand laid upon us, we need to be clear about what is being asked. As the account in Matthew makes evident, we are not being asked for a righteousness like that of the chief priests and the elders.

Ezekiel talks about the demand for righteousness, but the crucial thing is the turning away from wickedness and the striving for good. "Because he considered and turned away from all the transgressions which he had committed, he shall surely live, he shall not die."

Second Lesson: Phil. 2:1–13. In his letter to the Philippians, Paul wrote about the need to "work out your own salvation," and also gave some interpretation of what that might mean. One way to sum up what Paul is saying is in his admonition: "Have this mind among yourselves, which you have in Christ Jesus." We do not do what God asks of us by being obedient to a set of laws or adhering to a fixed standard of righteousness. Rather we are called to let our words and actions be informed by the mind of Christ, and to respond in every situation by expressing the spirit and the love of Christ.

We manifest that mind through the humility which willingly gives up prerogative and position even as Christ emptied himself, and through the humility which rejoices in the good in others. We manifest that mind through care and compassion for others even as Christ gave of himself for others, care and compassion which leads each person to "look not only to his own interests but also to the interests of others." We manifest that mind as we are willing to run the risks and accept the weaknesses of love, even as Christ ministered in the form of a servant and "became obedient unto death, even death upon a cross."

We live in the continuing paradox of God's grace and God's demands. What the Lord asks of us is the repentance which turns away from wickedness, and the righteousness which seeks to manifest the mind of Christ in our world.